ORIGINS of the COLD WAR

ORIGINS of the COLD WAR

The Novikov, Kennan, and Roberts
'Long Telegrams' of 1946

REVISED EDITION

WITH THREE NEW COMMENTARIES

Kenneth M. Jensen, Editor

UNITED STATES INSTITUTE OF PEACE PRESS
Washington, D.C.

United States Institute of Peace
1550 M Street, N.W.
Washington, D.C. 20005-1708

First edition published 1991
Revised edition published 1993

Printed in the United States of America

Library of Congress Cataloging-in-Publication Data
Origins of the Cold War: the Novikov, Kennan, and Roberts "long telegrams" of 1946 /
Kenneth M. Jensen, editor. — Rev. ed.
    p. cm.
    ISBN 1-878379-27-5 (pbk.)
    1. Cold War—Sources. I. Jensen, Kenneth M. (Kenneth Martin), 1944– .
D839.3.074 1993   93-43921
909.82'4—dc20   CIP

Contents

Preface to the Revised Edition

When the first edition of this collection was being prepared by the United States Institute of Peace in late 1990 and early 1991, Mikhail Gorbachev was still the leader of an intact Soviet Union. There were signs of change, of course—Eduard Shevardnadze had resigned as foreign minister; reactionary forces were jockeying with Gorbachev—but the rapid and dramatic changes that culminated in the August 1991 coup and December's dissolution of the Soviet Union were still a long way down the road. And though we anticipated more change ahead, we had no reason to believe that 1991 would differ so greatly from 1990.

As a consequence, we applauded the Soviet government's modest efforts toward openness that made possible our co-sponsored conference on the origins of the Cold War and brought to light the Novikov "Long Telegram." The conference was held in two meetings, in Moscow and in Washington, during the summer of 1990. At the time, we hoped that our successes in gaining materials from Soviet archives that were relevant to the history of U.S.-Soviet relations would lead to further work along the same lines. Shevardnadze's unilateral opening of the Foreign Ministry archives on August 18, 1990, certainly seemed to prepare the way for more effective access to documents that would lure Western scholars to Moscow and present numerous opportunities for joint work by Soviet and Western scholars.

In fact, of course, the remainder of 1991 played out rather differently than we, and most other observers, had anticipated. The Soviet political scene grew more problematic, and it was hardly the best of times for Soviets in charge of previously secret public records to advance the arduous and complicated task of turning their good intentions into useful retrieval systems and facilities. It was also hardly the best of times for Western scholars to visit the country for extended periods of work—or for Soviet scholars to go abroad. Still, new efforts were launched and professional contacts continued to be made. In the United States, a number of projects to assist the Soviets with the management of their archives and to conduct research in Moscow were begun or revitalized.

Events in Russia since August 1991 have been tumultuous and disruptive of our research objectives. But if they have not permitted rapid expansion of access to historical information, the openness that began during our experience in the summer of 1991 retains its promise. The demise of the Soviet Union, and especially of the Communist Party, has opened up to public access numerous sources of information, many more promising for Western historians of international relations than the Foreign Ministry archives. However, the burdens of making that opening meaningful have become far greater and more taxing at the very time when social and financial resources for new efforts in scholarship and information sharing have become notably more scarce.

Today we assume that it may be a long time before convenient access to Soviet archives will enable historians to further advance the project of understanding the history of Soviet and Western relations. Nonetheless, we offer this revised edition of *Origins of the Cold War* in the same spirit as the first: in the hope that it will encourage scholars and students to pursue this important historical project with as much vigor as possible under the circumstances.

The Revised Edition

When the original volume was in preparation, the Institute made available to the editors of the journal *Diplomatic History* its translation of the Novikov document for purposes of generating a symposium on "The Soviet Side of the Cold War." When the papers from that symposium appeared in the Fall 1991 issue of the journal, we realized that the Institute could significantly improve its original effort by including in a new edition several of the *Diplomatic History* commentaries, since they shed new light on the origins of the Novikov document and provided context and perspectives useful in its analysis.

Two of the contributors to the *Diplomatic History* symposium, Viktor Mal'kov and Melvyn Leffler, had participated in our summer 1990 conference. Mal'kov, from the Institute of World History of the Academy of Sciences in Moscow, subsequently undertook research on the origins of the Novikov document. (As the preface to the first edition indicates, this research had not been done at the time the document was given to the Institute.) Mal'kov drew on Novikov's memoirs, published in Moscow in 1989, and on a number of archival sources to reveal Molotov's role in the creation of the document and the document's subsequent role in early Soviet Cold War policy deliberations.

For his part, Leffler, a professor of history at the University of Virginia, took advantage of the time immediately after our conference to reflect on a number of important matters, including the extent to which Novikov's analysis stood up to the actual facts of Western attitudes and actions and the degree to which the "symptoms" of the building Cold War mentality—both East and West—are evidenced by Novikov's approach and conclusions.

A third contributor to the *Diplomatic History* effort, Steven Miner—an Ohio University history professor engaged at the time in the study of U.S.-Soviet diplomacy during World War II—brought to the symposium a most useful perspective on the limits of analyzing thinking in Moscow during 1946 (and later) on the basis of such partial evidence as the Novikov document. Miner's commentary—like Leffler's—should be kept in mind by new students of the early Cold War period as they turn for the first time to the Novikov document and other purportedly significant Soviet archival materials that may eventually appear.

We would like to thank the editors of *Diplomatic History* for permitting the inclusion of these three commentaries in this edition of *Origins of the Cold War*.

The ultimate significance of the Novikov "Long Telegram" is yet to be determined. Historian John Lewis Gaddis, introducing the *Diplomatic History* symposium in the fall of 1991, welcomed the publication of the Novikov document but lamented that it provided "a woefully inadequate basis for beginning the daunting exercise of writing 'the other side' of Cold War history." As noted above, work on "the other side" has moved forward over the past several years, but the project proceeds still on "woefully inadequate" bases.

Revising a book like this one thus has its hazards. Today, in the fall of 1993, with the struggle for democracy and reform in Russia still in an uncertain state, the sense of hazard is especially acute. Fortunately for the historian, however, even if the present environment changes, documents like those included in this book do not. The Institute once again commends the "Long Telegrams" of 1946—and the study of Cold War history—to scholars, teachers, students, and other interested readers. Now, perhaps even more than in 1990 and 1991, a clear understanding of the history of East-West relations is vital to the building of new relations between Russia and the West and to the new cooperative international endeavors that have brought hope—and substantial new complexity—to the post–Cold War world.

Richard H. Solomon
President
November 1993

Preface

During June and July 1990, the United States Institute of Peace and the Research Coordination Center of the Soviet Ministry of Foreign Affairs conducted a seminar for American and Soviet historians in Moscow and in Washington on the origins of the Cold War. During the Washington sessions, the chairman of the Soviet group, Vladimir Shustov, presented a copy of a previously unpublished cable sent by Soviet Ambassador to the United States Nikolai Novikov to Foreign Minister Viacheslav Molotov on September 27, 1946. The Soviet chairman suggested that the Novikov cable in some ways might be parallel to the famous "Long Telegram" sent by U.S. Chargé d'Affaires George Kennan from Moscow to the Department of State earlier in the same year.

Ambassador Shustov indicated his sense of the Novikov telegram's potential significance by stating that the Foreign Ministry intended to publish it. In Shustov's opinion, the Novikov cable, newly discovered in the archives of the Soviet Foreign Ministry, had been important to Molotov in his deliberations on the course of Soviet foreign policy, as he had indicated that it should be kept in his personal files until January 1, 1947. Shustov also said that the Novikov cable was "in a way parallel to Kennan's famous cable of mid-February."

Kennan's cable, which was sent on February 22, 1946, is rightly regarded as one of the landmark documents of the early Cold War period. It contained persuasive analysis of Soviet history, society, outlook, and intentions that influenced U.S. policy toward the Soviet Union for years thereafter and provided the intellectual underpinning for what came to be known as the policy of "containment." Like the 1950 National Security Council Memorandum No. 68 (NSC-68), which spelled out the implications of the containment policy for U.S. foreign policy, defense, and security agencies, the Kennan telegram has been studied and re-studied well into the era of glasnost and perestroika and will be the subject of historical inquiry for some time to come.

In comparing the Novikov cable to the Kennan "Long Telegram," Ambassador Shustov offered the Novikov cable as a potentially significant Cold War document. Whether or not it was will take some time to determine. As with any such diplomatic message, its place in a series of documents and events must be established to determine its role and the extent of its influence. Because the early history of the Cold War has been so thoroughly researched on the U.S. side, we have a very good idea regarding the influence of Kennan and his "Long Telegram." Soviet research on the origins of the Cold War is just beginning in earnest. Consequently, there are no firm answers yet to such questions as how Novikov figured in the constellation of Soviet foreign actors; how such cables from Soviet missions figured in policymaking; or whether Novikov was telling Stalin and Molotov something they wanted to hear from their subordinates or something, in Novikov's view, they needed to hear.

The Soviet Foreign Ministry published the Novikov cable, alongside the Kennan "Long Telegram," in the November 1990 issue of *Mezhdunarodnaia zhizn'*, an official publication of the Foreign Ministry. To the best of our knowledge, the present volume contains the first publication of the Novikov telegram outside the Soviet Union. Rather than conduct a detailed and time-consuming analysis of the document and present its findings along with the text of the cable, we decided that publication should come as quickly as possible to get the telegram into circulation for historians. Rendered in English translation, as it is here, the Novikov cable will be accessible to a wider range of scholars and analysts than would otherwise be the case.

We thought that it would be useful to set Novikov's cable alongside several other early Cold War documents of a similar sort. The most obvious document to include was Kennan's "Long Telegram." Given the role of the British in the development of East-West relations after World War II, we thought it would be appropriate to include along with the Novikov and Kennan telegrams a series of three cables by Britain's chargé d'affaires in Moscow, Frank Roberts, that was sent to Foreign Minister Ernest Bevin during March 1946. Like the Novikov document, these cables have been compared to the Kennan "Long Telegram." [For more on the Roberts documents, see Sean Greenwood, "Frank Roberts and the 'Other' Long Telegram: The View from the British Embassy in Moscow, March 1946," *Journal of Contemporary History* 25 (London: Sage Publishing Inc., 1990), 103-22.]

Taken together, the Novikov, Kennan, and Roberts documents allow the reader the opportunity to make comparisons among U.S., Soviet, and British thinking in 1946. Irrespective of one's prior knowledge of this period, all of these cables are informative and fascinating. Needless to say, the Institute does not assert that these documents are necessarily equivalent—or, as Vladimir Shustov put it, "parallel"—in style, substance, or significance. How they come to be regarded with respect to one another is up to historians and other scholars.

United States Institute of Peace–Soviet Foreign Ministry Seminar on the Origins of the Cold War

The story of how the Novikov "Long Telegram" came into the hands of the United States Institute of Peace (and, therewith, into this publication) is in itself an event in the history of the Cold War, in particular with regard to its demise.

The seminar on the origins of the Cold War stemmed from discussions in 1989 between U.S. Assistant Secretary of State for Human Rights Richard Schifter, an ex officio member of the Institute's Board of Directors, and (then) Soviet Deputy Foreign Minister Anatoly Adamishin. In informal conversations about the aftermath of World War II, in the context of the end of the Cold War, the two came to agree that there was a lack of mutual understanding of the origins of U.S.-Soviet tensions spanning the last 45 years. They decided that it was time for the United States and the Soviet Union to begin to bridge this gap.

At the same time Schifter and Adamishin were discussing the lack of a common history, Soviet authorities and scholars within and outside the Soviet Union were beginning a campaign to open

Soviet archives. A number of important Soviet documents had been released and published in official organs, most notably the Hitler-Stalin (Molotov-Ribbentrop) Pact of 1939. In the fall of 1989, legislation to open archival holdings more than thirty years old was prepared for submission to the Supreme Soviet. Although at this writing such legislation has not been acted upon, the push for open archives has continued. In considering a new U.S.-Soviet look at the origins of the Cold War, both the Institute and the Foreign Ministry's Research Coordination Center committed themselves to the principle of free access to public documents and to encouraging the opening of Soviet and other archives.

Negotiations proceeded between the United States Institute of Peace and the Foreign Ministry during the fall and winter of 1989-90. In early spring 1990 a design was drawn up for a modest seminar to be jointly conducted by the Institute and the Research Coordination Center, a new entity within the Foreign Ministry charged with enhancing the role of objective research in Soviet foreign policy. It was decided that groups of American and Soviet scholars would meet in Moscow during the last week of June and again in the last week in July in Washington. Topics to be discussed included the state of Cold War historiography; Soviet-American relations, 1917-45; the wartime-postwar settlement: diplomacy at Yalta and Potsdam; the Pacific War, 1945; the creation and use of nuclear weapons; domestic factors and the origins of the Cold War; consolidation of the Cold War, 1945-50; and lessons of the origins of the Cold War.

Scholars were then selected. The American group included Professor Allen Weinstein (chairman), an eminent historian who is a member of the Institute's Board of Directors; former United States Secretary of Defense Clark Clifford (special guest at the Washington sessions); Mr. Robert Conquest (Moscow sessions only); Dr. Francis Fukuyama; Professor John Gaddis; Dr. Kenneth M. Jensen; Mr. Walter Laqueur (Moscow sessions only); Professor Melvyn Leffler; Ambassador Samuel W. Lewis; Ambassador Paul Nitze (Washington sessions only); Professor Richard Pipes; Professor Elspeth Davies Rostow; Professor Walt Whitman Rostow; Assistant Secretary of State Richard Schifter; Professor Arthur M. Schlesinger, Jr.; Professor Gaddis Smith (Washington sessions only); Mr. Helmut Sonnenfeldt (Washington sessions only); Professor W. Scott Thompson; and Professor Adam Ulam (Washington sessions only).

The Soviet group included Ambassador Vladimir V. Shustov (chairman); Dr. Aleksandr O. Chubar'ian; Dr. Aleksei M. Filitov; Dr. Viktor L. Mal'kov; Dr. Mikhail M. Narinskii; Deputy Foreign Minister Aleksei Obukhov; Dr. Vladimir Pechatnov (Washington sessions only); Dr. Sergei Plekhanov; Dr. Konstantin Pleshakov; Dr. Yurii A. Poliakov; Vladimir Sokolov (Washington sessions only); and Dr. Vladislav Zubok.

The Moscow sessions of the seminar were held south of the city at Meshcherino, a group of dachas belonging to the Foreign Ministry. Three days of paper presentations and discussion were interspersed and followed by press conferences and meetings with Soviet scholars and officials in Moscow. The U.S. and Soviet groups met with Evgenii Primakov, a member of Mikhail Gorbachev's Presidential Council, in his Kremlin office for two hours, and with Foreign Minister Eduard Shevardnadze at the ministry for more than an hour. Deputy Foreign Minister Obukhov, who took part in the seminar, and Deputy Foreign Minister Petrovskii sponsored dinners for the participants, as did U.S. Ambassador to the Soviet Union Jack Matlock. The seminar received wide coverage by the Soviet and international media.

The Washington sessions of the seminar were held at the United States Institute of Peace and other venues. Two days of discussion continued the scholarly dialogue begun in Moscow. A briefing was held at the National Press Club and was shown on C-SPAN, and participants took part in meetings at the National Archives (hosted by U.S. Archivist Donald Wilson), the Library of Congress (hosted by Librarian of Congress James Billington), and the Department of State and on Capitol Hill (hosted by Allen Weinstein and the Center for Democracy).

The scholars were also received by (then) Acting Secretary of State Lawrence Eagleburger, who discussed future relations between the United States and the Soviet Union and other issues with them for nearly an hour and a half. Dinners were held for the participants by Ambassador Richard Schifter, Institute Board Member W. Scott Thompson, and Soviet Chargé d'Affaires Sergei Chetverikov. The Washington sessions closed with a dinner at the Mayflower Hotel at which Ambassador Paul Nitze and Representative Jim Leach spoke.

All the Moscow and Washington sessions of the seminar were intense and lively. While new information (particularly from the Soviet side, as the presence of the Novikov cable in this volume suggests) was exchanged, the meetings were principally characterized by a call for more research and for new ways of thinking about events that launched the Cold War. The Soviet historians present frequently referred to the history of the Cold War as a complicated mosaic, many missing pieces of which will be put into place as they are discovered in Soviet archives. They called for joint research efforts between Soviet and Western scholars to locate the missing pieces. At the same time, the Soviets noted that this in itself would not be enough: new thinking had to ensue, and Western historians could help their Soviet colleagues immeasurably in "preparing proper tools of analysis."

One event during the seminar testified particularly clearly not only to its importance for the participants but to the importance to both the Soviet Union and the West of completing and reanalyzing the history of the Cold War. During his meeting with seminar participants, Soviet Foreign Minister Eduard Shevardnadze said that, in the pursuit of peace between the United States and the Soviet Union, one must not only take public opinion into account but be led by it. "Scientists" (that is, professional historians) are of the greatest importance in shaping public opinion, he said, implying that public understanding of the Cold War is critically important to good future relations between the two countries and that historians, more than others, will shape that public understanding.

To Western ears, this argument may sound rather unusual, since Communist party members customarily speak of the party as leading public opinion, rather than the reverse. Shevardnadze's comments, however, reflect the different situation that now exists in the Soviet Union. If glasnost has created an enthusiasm for anything among Soviet citizens, it is an enthusiasm for reevaluating the past. What the Soviet Union should become in the future is preeminently a matter of overcoming the past—something that cannot be done without understanding it.

That the history of the Cold War is of new and very significant interest to the Soviets surely makes it of new and very significant interest to the West. By the end of the sessions, it had become the hope of the seminar participants—U.S. and Soviet alike—that the joint study of the Cold War would lead to an objective, "scientific" history of U.S.-Soviet affairs that would contribute to the new relationship between the countries.

It was in this context that Ambassador Shustov offered the Novikov long telegram to the seminar participants. In his remarks, he stressed that the offering was made to show that Soviet intentions regarding the archives were in earnest. He wanted everyone present to understand that, by producing the Novikov document, the Soviet government was not making either a dramatic or a partial gesture. He remarked that it was not the Soviet intention to open archives "in a piecemeal approach." Here, Shustov appeared to be anticipating the possible accusation that the Foreign Ministry intended to "manage" information coming out of its archives.

That the Foreign Ministry favors free access to its archival holdings has been borne out by events. We are pleased to note here that the Soviet Foreign Ministry opened its archives on August 18, 1990 (a matter of weeks following the conclusion of our discussions), an action taken prior to the passage of any new Soviet law regarding archival materials.

Coming as it does at the beginning of a new era in Soviet historical scholarship, we hope that this publication will encourage scholars, teachers, students, and all interested readers to study the history of the Cold War while looking toward a future in which U.S.-Soviet relations are based on a new model of peaceful cooperation. It is our hope that this volume will find a wide audience. As the Cold War winds down, it is especially important not to lose sight of the fact that its full history has yet to be studied. And as Soviet Foreign Minister Eduard Shevardnadze reminded the participants in the Origins of the Cold War seminar, the future of Soviet-American relations depends a good deal on a clear and objective understanding of the history of those relations.

Samuel W. Lewis
President
February 1991

Editor's Note

The translation of the Novikov telegram was initially undertaken by Dr. John Glad, who also served as a simultaneous translator during the Washington sessions of the Origins of the Cold War seminar. This translation was thereafter revised, annotated, and otherwise prepared for publication by the editor of this volume. Although some of the references in the text have been amplified (with editorial additions set in brackets), the document is presented in English in a manner as close as possible to the Russian original. As the reader will see, we have reproduced Foreign Minister Molotov's underlinings in the document. Other markings are described in the footnotes. Generally speaking, they are checks or lines in the margin, indicating attention to whole sentences or to portions of paragraphs.

Beyond the treatment noted above, we have left the Novikov document unannotated. By and large, the facts and events cited by Novikov were a matter of public knowledge at the time. The interested reader can easily look them up in any of a large number of historical treatments of the period, including the many books by seminar participants John Lewis Gaddis and Adam Ulam. Because of this, and our desire to get the Novikov document into circulation in English as soon as possible, we have not annotated the document to explain facts and events cited.

The Kennan document is reproduced as it appeared in *Foreign Relations*, 1946, Volume VI: *Eastern Europe; The Soviet Union*, pages 696-709 (Washington, D.C.: United States Government Printing Office, 1969). This publication contains some amplifications provided by the journal editors. The document should therefore not be taken to replicate the original. Furthermore, we have made a few minor editorial changes to improve readability.

The Roberts documents are presented as they appear in the files of the British Public Record Office (Frank Roberts to FO, 14, 17, and 18 March 1946, FO 371 56763 N4065/4156/4157/38, Public Record Office, London), except for a few minor editorial changes.

The editor wishes to thank Kimber M. Schraub and Aileen C. Hefferren for their work in preparing the manuscript, Joan Engelhardt for production management, and Marie Marr-Williams for manuscript tracking. A special note of thanks goes to the Institute's reference librarian, Denise Dowdell, for help in securing the Kennan and Roberts documents.

Kenneth M. Jensen

The Telegrams

The Novikov Telegram

Washington, September 27, 1946

U.S. Foreign Policy in the Postwar Period[1]

[All underlining replicates that of Foreign Minister Viacheslav Molotov.]

The foreign policy of the United States, which reflects the imperialist tendencies of American monopolistic capital, is characterized in the postwar period by a striving <u>for world supremacy</u>.[2] This is the real meaning of the many statements by President Truman and other representatives of American ruling circles: that the United States has the right to lead the world. All the forces of American diplomacy—the army, the air force, the navy, industry, and science—are enlisted in the service of this foreign policy. For this purpose broad plans for expansion have been developed and are being implemented through diplomacy and the establishment of a system of naval and air bases stretching far beyond the boundaries of the United States, through the arms race, and through the creation of ever newer types of weapons.

1. a) The foreign policy of the United States is conducted now <u>in a situation that differs greatly</u> from the one that existed in the prewar period. This situation does not fully conform to the calculations of those reactionary circles which hoped that during the Second World War they would succeed in avoiding, at least for a long time, the main battles in Europe and Asia. They calculated that the United States of America, if it was unsuccessful in completely avoiding direct participation in the war, would enter it

3

only at the last minute, when it could easily affect the outcome of the war, completely ensuring its interests.

In this regard, it was thought that the main competitors of the United States would be crushed or greatly weakened in the war, and the United States by virtue of this circumstance would assume the role of the most powerful factor in resolving the fundamental questions of the postwar world. These calculations were also based on the assumption, which was very widespread in the United States in the initial stages of the war, that the Soviet Union, which had been subjected to the attack of German Fascism in June 1941, would also be exhausted or even completely destroyed as a result of the war.

Reality did not bear out the calculations of the American imperialists.

b) The two main aggressive powers, fascist Germany and militarist Japan, which were at the same time the main competitors of the United States in both the economic and foreign policy fields, were thoroughly defeated. The third great power, Great Britain, which had taken heavy blows during the war, now faces enormous economic and political difficulties. The political foundations of the British Empire were appreciably shaken, and crises arose, for example, in India, Palestine, and Egypt.

Europe has come out of the war with a completely dislocated economy, and the economic devastation that occurred in the course of the war cannot be overcome in a short time. All of the countries of Europe and Asia are experiencing a colossal need for consumer goods, industrial and transportation equipment, etc. Such a situation provides American monopolistic capital with prospects for enormous shipments of goods and the importation of capital into these countries—a circumstance that would permit it to infiltrate their national economies.

Such a development would mean a serious strengthening of the economic position of the United States in the whole world and would be a stage on the road to world domination by the United States.

c) On the other hand, we have seen a failure of calculations on the part of U.S. circles which assumed that the Soviet Union would be destroyed in the war or would come out of it so weakened that it would be forced to go begging to the United States for economic assistance. Had that happened, they would have been able to dictate conditions permitting the United States to carry out its expansion in Europe and Asia without hindrance from the USSR.

In actuality, despite all of the economic difficulties of the postwar period connected with the enormous losses inflicted by the war and the German fascist occupation, the Soviet Union continues to remain economically independent of the outside world and is rebuilding its national economy with its own forces.

At the same time the USSR's international position is currently stronger than it was in the prewar period. Thanks to the historical victories of Soviet weapons, the Soviet armed forces are located on the territory of Germany and other formerly hostile countries, thus guaranteeing that these countries will not be used again for an attack on the USSR. In formerly hostile countries, such as Bulgaria, Finland, Hungary, and Romania, democratic reconstruction has established regimes that have undertaken to strengthen and maintain friendly relations with the Soviet Union. In the Slavic countries that were liberated by the Red Army or with its assistance—Poland, Czechoslovakia, and Yugoslavia—democratic regimes have also been established that maintain relations with the Soviet Union on the basis of agreements on friendship and mutual assistance.

The enormous relative weight of the USSR in international affairs in general and in the European countries in particular, the independence of its foreign policy, and the economic and political assistance that it provides to neighboring countries, both allies and former enemies, has led to the growth of the political influence of the Soviet Union in these countries and to the further strengthening of democratic tendencies in them.

Such a situation in Eastern and Southeastern Europe cannot help but be regarded by the American imperialists as an obstacle in the path of the expansionist policy of the United States.

2. a) The foreign policy of the United States is not determined at present by the circles in the Democratic party that (as was the case during Roosevelt's lifetime) strive to strengthen the cooperation of the three great powers that constituted the basis of the anti-Hitler coalition during the war. The ascendance to power of President Truman, a politically unstable person but with certain conservative tendencies, and the subsequent appointment of [James] Byrnes as Secretary of State meant a strengthening of the

influence on U.S. foreign policy of the most reactionary circles of the Democratic party. The constantly increasing reactionary nature of the foreign policy course of the United States, which consequently approached the policy advocated by the Republican party, laid the groundwork for close cooperation in this field between the far right wing of the Democratic party and the Republican party. This cooperation of the two parties, which took shape in both houses of Congress in the form of an unofficial bloc of reactionary Southern Democrats and the old guard of the Republicans headed by [Senator Arthur] Vandenberg and [Senator Robert] Taft, was especially clearly manifested in the essentially identical foreign policy statements issued by figures of both parties. In Congress and at international conferences, where as a rule leading Republicans are represented in the delegations of the United States, the Republicans actively support the foreign policy of the government. This is the source of what is called, even in official statements, "bi-partisan" foreign policy.

b) At the same time, there has been a decline in the influence on foreign policy of those who follow Roosevelt's course for cooperation among peace-loving countries.[3] Such persons in the government, in Congress, and in the leadership of the Democratic party are being pushed farther and farther into the background. The contradictions in the field of foreign policy existing between the followers of [Henry] Wallace and [Claude] Pepper, on the one hand, and the adherents of the reactionary "bi-partisan" policy, on the other, were manifested with great clarity recently in the speech by Wallace that led to his resignation from the post of Secretary of Commerce. Wallace's resignation means the victory of the reactionary course that Byrnes is conducting in cooperation with Vandenberg and Taft.

3. Obvious indications of the U.S. effort to establish world dominance are also to be found in the increase in military potential in peacetime and in the establishment of a large number of naval and air bases both in the United States and beyond its borders.

In the summer of 1946, for the first time in the history of the country, Congress passed a law on the establishment of a peacetime army, not on a volunteer basis but on the basis of universal military service. The size of the army, which is supposed to amount to about one million persons as of July 1, 1947, was also increased significantly. The size of the navy at the conclusion of the war decreased quite insignificantly in comparison with wartime. At the present time, the American navy occupies first place in the world, leaving England's navy far behind, to say nothing of those of other countries.

Expenditures on the army and navy have risen colossally, amounting to 13 billion dollars according to the budget for 1946-47 (about 40 percent of the total budget of 36 billion dollars). This is more than ten times greater than corresponding expenditures in the budget for 1938, which did not amount to even one billion dollars.

Along with maintaining a large army, navy, and air force, the budget provides that these enormous amounts also will be spent on establishing a very extensive system of naval and air bases in the Atlantic and Pacific oceans. According to existing official plans, in the course of the next few years 228 bases, points of support, and radio stations are to be constructed in the Atlantic Ocean and 258 in the Pacific. A large number of these bases and points of support are located outside the boundaries of the United States. In the Atlantic Ocean bases exist or are under construction in the following foreign island territories: Newfoundland, Iceland, Cuba, Trinidad, Bermuda, the Bahamas, the Azores, and many others; in the Pacific Ocean: former Japanese mandated territories—the Marianas, Caroline and Marshall Islands, Bonin, Ryukyu, Philippines, and the Galapagos Islands (they belong to Ecuador).

The establishment of American bases on islands that are often 10,000 to 12,000 kilometers from the territory of the United States and are on the other side of the Atlantic and Pacific oceans clearly indicates the offensive nature of the strategic concepts of the commands of the U.S. army and navy. This interpretation is also confirmed by the fact that the American navy is intensively studying the naval approaches to the boundaries of Europe. For this purpose, American naval vessels in the course of 1946 visited the ports of Norway, Denmark, Sweden, Turkey, and Greece. In addition, the American navy is constantly operating in the Mediterranean Sea.

All of these facts show clearly that a decisive role in the realization of plans for world dominance by the United States is played by its armed forces.

4. a) One of the stages in the achievement of dominance over the world by the United States is its <u>understanding with England</u> <u>concerning the partial division of the world on the basis of mutual</u> <u>concessions</u>.[4] The basic lines of the secret agreement between the United States and England regarding the division of the world consist, as shown by facts, in their agreement on the inclusion of Japan and China in the sphere of influence of the United States in the Far East, while the United States, for its part, has agreed not to hinder England either in resolving the Indian problem or in strengthening its influence in Siam and Indonesia.

b) In connection with this division, the United States at the present time is in control of China and Japan without any interference from England.

The American policy <u>in China</u> is striving for the complete economic and political submission of China to the control of American monopolistic capital. Following this policy, the American government does not shrink even from interference in the internal affairs of China. At the present time in China, there are more than 50,000 American soldiers. In a number of cases, American Marines participated directly in military operations against the people's liberation forces. The so-called "mediation" mission of General [George] Marshall is only a cover for interference in the internal affairs of China.

How far the policy of the American government has gone with regard to China is indicated by the fact that at present it is striving to effect control over China's army. Recently, the U.S. administration submitted to Congress a bill on military assistance to China that provided for the complete reorganization of the Chinese army, its training with the aid of U.S. military instructors, and its supply with American weapons and equipment.[5] For the purpose of carrying out this program in China, an American consultative mission including army and naval officers would be sent to China.

China is gradually being transformed into a bridgehead for the American armed forces. American air bases are located all over its territory. The main ones are found in Peking, Tsingtao, Tientsin, Nanking, Shanghai, Chendu, Chungking, and Kunming. The main American naval base in China is located in Tsingtao. The headquarters of the 7th Fleet is also there. In addition more than 30,000 U.S. Marines are concentrated in Tsingtao and its environs.

The measures carried out in northern China by the American army show that it intends to stay there for a long time.

In Japan, despite the presence there of only a small contingent of American troops, control is in the hands of the Americans. Although English capital has substantial interests in the Japanese economy, English foreign policy toward Japan is conducted in such a way as not to hinder the Americans from carrying out their penetration of the Japanese national economy and subordinating it to their influence. In the Far Eastern Commission in Washington and in the Allied Council in Tokyo, the English representatives as a rule make common cause with the U.S. representatives conducting this policy.

Measures taken by the American occupational authorities in the area of domestic policy and intended to support reactionary classes and groups, which the United States plans to use in the struggle against the Soviet Union, also meet with a sympathetic attitude on the part of England.

c) The United States follows a similar line with regard to the English sphere of influence in the Far East. Recently, the United States has ceased the attempts it has made over the past year to influence the resolution of Indian questions. Lately there have been frequent instances in which the reputable American press, more or less faithfully reflecting the official policy of the U.S. government, has made positive statements with regard to the English policy in India. American foreign policy also did not hinder British troops in joint action with the Dutch army from suppressing the national liberation movement in Indonesia. Moreover, there have even been instances in which the United States facilitated this British imperialist policy, handing over American weapons and equipment to the English and Dutch troops in Indonesia, sending Dutch naval personnel from the United States to Indonesia, etc.

5. a) If the division of the world in the Far East between the United States and England may be considered an accomplished fact, it cannot be said that an analogous situation exists in the basin of the Mediterranean Sea and in the countries adjacent to it.[6] Rather, the facts indicate that an agreement of this sort has not yet been reached in the region of the Near East and the Mediterranean Sea. The difficulty experienced by the United States and England in reaching an agreement over this region derives from the fact

that concessions on the part of England to the United States in the Mediterranean basin would be fraught with serious consequences for the whole future of the British Empire, for which the basin has exceptional strategic and economic significance. England would have nothing against using American armed forces and influence in this region, directing them northward against the Soviet Union. The United States, however, is not interested in providing assistance and support to the British Empire in this vulnerable point, but rather in its own more thorough penetration of the Mediterranean basin and Near East, to which the United States is attracted by the area's natural resources, primarily oil.

b) In recent years American capital has penetrated very intensively into the economy of the Near Eastern countries, in particular into the oil industry. At present there are American oil concessions in all of the Near Eastern countries that have oil deposits (Iraq, Bahrain, Kuwait, Egypt, and Saudi Arabia). American capital, which made its first appearance in the oil industry of the Near East only in 1927, now controls about 42 percent of all proven reserves in the Near East, excluding Iran. Of the total proven reserves of 26.8 billion barrels, over 11 billion barrels are owned by U.S. concessions. Striving to ensure further development of their concessions in different countries (which are often very large—Saudi Arabia, for example), the American oil companies plan to build a trans-Arabian pipeline to transport oil from the American concession in Saudi Arabia and in other countries on the southeastern shore of the Mediterranean Sea to ports in Palestine and Egypt.

In expanding in the Near East, American capital has English capital as its greatest and most stubborn competitor. The fierce competition between them is the chief factor preventing England and the United States from reaching an understanding on the division of spheres of influence in the Near East, a division that can occur only at the expense of direct British interests in this region.

Palestine is an example of the very acute contradictions in the policy of the United States and England in the Near East. The United States has been displaying great initiative there of late, creating many difficulties for England, as in the case of the U.S. demand that 100,000 Jews from Europe be permitted to enter Palestine. The American interest in Palestine, outwardly expressed as sympathy for the Zionist cause, actually only signifies that American capital wishes to interfere in Palestinian affairs and thus penetrate the economy. The selection of a port in Palestine as one of the terminal points of the American oil pipeline explains a great deal regarding the foreign policy of the United States on the Palestine question.

c) The irregular nature of relations between England and the United States in the Near East is manifested in part also in the great activity of the American naval fleet in the eastern part of the Mediterranean Sea. Such activity cannot help but be in conflict with the basic interests of the British Empire. These actions on the part of the U.S. fleet undoubtedly are also linked with American oil and other economic interests in the Near East.

It must be kept in mind, however, that incidents such as the visit by the American battleship *Missouri* to the Black Sea straits, the visit of the American fleet to Greece, and the great interest that U.S. diplomacy displays in the problem of the straits have a double meaning. On the one hand, they indicate that the United States has decided to consolidate its position in the Mediterranean basin to support its interests in the countries of the Near East and that it has selected the navy as the tool for this policy. On the other hand, these incidents constitute a political and military demonstration against the Soviet Union. The strengthening of U.S. positions in the Near East and the establishment of conditions for basing the American navy at one or more points on the Mediterranean Sea (Trieste, Palestine, Greece, Turkey) will therefore signify the emergence of a new threat to the security of the southern regions of the Soviet Union.

6. a) Relations between the United States and England are determined by two basic circumstances.[7] On the one hand, the United States regards England as its greatest potential competitor; on the other hand, England constitutes a possible ally for the United States. Division of certain regions of the globe into spheres of influence of the United States and England would create the opportunity, if not for preventing competition between them, which is impossible, then at least of reducing it. At the same time, such a division facilitates the achievement of economic and political cooperation between them.

b) England needs American credits for reorganizing its economy, which was disrupted by the war. To obtain such credits

England is compelled to make significant concessions. This is the significance of the loan that the United States recently granted England. With the aid of the loan, England can strengthen its economy. At the same time this loan opens the door for American capital to penetrate the British Empire. The narrow bounds in which the trade of the so-called Sterling Bloc has found itself in the recent past have expanded at the present time and provide an opportunity for the Americans to trade with British dominions, India, and other countries of the Sterling Bloc (Egypt, Iraq, and Palestine).

c) The political support that the United States provides for England is very often manifested in the international events of the postwar period. At recent international conferences the United States and England have closely coordinated their policies, especially in cases when they had to oppose the policy of the Soviet Union. The United States provided moral and political assistance to England in the latter's reactionary policy in Greece, India, and Indonesia. American and English policy is fully coordinated with regard to the Slavic and other countries adjoining the Soviet Union. The most important *démarches* of the United States and England in these countries after the end of the war were quite similar and parallel in nature. The policy of the United States and England in the Security Council of the United Nations (particularly in questions concerning Iran, Spain, Greece, the withdrawal of foreign troops from Syria and Lebanon, etc.) has the same features of coordination.

d) The ruling circles of the United States obviously have a sympathetic attitude toward the idea of a military alliance with England, but at the present time the matter has not yet culminated in an official alliance. Churchill's speech in Fulton calling for the conclusion of an Anglo-American military alliance for the purpose of establishing joint domination over the world was therefore not supported officially by Truman or Byrnes, although Truman by his presence [during the "Iron Curtain" speech] did indirectly sanction Churchill's appeal.

Even if the United States does not go so far as to conclude a military alliance with England just now, in practice they still maintain very close contact on military questions. The combined Anglo-American headquarters in Washington continues to exist, despite the fact that over a year has passed since the end of the war. Frequent personal contact continues among leading military figures of England and the United States. The recent trip of Field Marshal Montgomery to America is evidence of this contact. It is characteristic that as a result of his meetings with leading military figures of the United States, Montgomery announced that the English army would be structured on the American model.[8] Cooperation is also carried out between the navies of the two countries. In this connection it is sufficient to note the participation of the English navy in recent maneuvers by the American navy in the Mediterranean Sea and the participation by the American navy in the North Sea in autumn of this year.

e) The current relations between England and the United States, despite the temporary attainment of agreements on very important questions, are plagued with great internal contradictions and cannot be lasting.

The economic assistance from the United States conceals within itself a danger for England in many respects. First of all, in accepting the loan, England finds herself in a certain financial dependence on the United States from which it will not be easy to free herself. Second, it should be kept in mind that the conditions created by the loan for the penetration by American capital of the British Empire can entail serious political consequences. The countries included in the British Empire or dependent on it may— under economic pressure from powerful American capital— reorient themselves toward the United States, following in this respect the example of Canada, which more and more is moving away from the influence of England and orienting itself toward the United States. The strengthening of American positions in the Far East could stimulate a similar process in Australia and New Zealand. In the Arabic countries of the Near East, which are striving to emancipate themselves from the British Empire, there are groups within the ruling circles that would not be averse to working out a deal with the United States. It is quite possible that the Near East will become a center of Anglo-American contradictions that will explode the agreements now reached between the United States and England.[9]

7. a) The "hard-line" policy with regard to the USSR announced by Byrnes after the rapprochement of the reactionary Democrats with the Republicans is at present the main obstacle on the road to cooperation of the Great Powers.[10] It consists

mainly of the fact that in the postwar period the United States no longer follows a policy of strengthening cooperation among the Big Three (or Four) but rather has striven to undermine the unity of these countries. The objective has been to impose the will of other countries on the Soviet Union. This is precisely the tenor of the policy of certain countries, which is being carried out with the blessing of the United States, to undermine or completely abolish the principle of the veto in the Security Council of the United Nations. This would give the United States opportunities to form among the Great Powers narrow groupings and blocs directed primarily against the Soviet Union, and thus to split the United Nations. Rejection of the veto by the Great Powers would transform the United Nations into an Anglo-Saxon domain in which the United States would play the leading role.

b) The present policy of the American government with regard to the USSR is also directed at limiting or dislodging the influence of the Soviet Union from neighboring countries. In implementing this policy in former enemy or Allied countries adjacent to the USSR, the United States attempts, at various international conferences or directly in these countries themselves, to support reactionary forces with the purpose of creating obstacles to the process of democratization of these countries. In so doing, it also attempts to secure positions for the penetration of American capital into their economies. Such a policy is intended to weaken and overthrow the democratic governments in power there, which are friendly toward the USSR, and replace them in the future with new governments that would obediently carry out a policy dictated from the United States. In this policy, the United States receives full support from English diplomacy.

c) One of the most important elements in the general policy of the United States, which is directed toward limiting the international role of the USSR in the postwar world, is the policy with regard to Germany. In Germany, the United States is taking measures to strengthen reactionary forces for the purpose of opposing democratic reconstruction. Furthermore, it displays special insistence on accompanying this policy with completely inadequate measures for the demilitarization of Germany.

The American occupation policy does not have the objective of eliminating the remnants of German Fascism and rebuilding German political life on a democratic basis, so that Germany might cease to exist as an aggressive force. The United States is not taking measures to eliminate the monopolistic associations of German industrialists on which German Fascism depended in preparing aggression and waging war. Neither is any agrarian reform being conducted to eliminate large landholders, who were also a reliable support for the Hitlerites. Instead, the United States is considering the possibility of terminating the Allied occupation of German territory before the main tasks of the occupation—the demilitarization and democratization of Germany—have been implemented. This would create the prerequisites for the revival of an imperialist Germany, which the United States plans to use in a future war on its side. One cannot help seeing that such a policy has a clearly outlined anti-Soviet edge and constitutes a serious danger to the cause of peace.

d) The numerous and extremely hostile statements by American government, political, and military figures with regard to the Soviet Union and its foreign policy are very characteristic of the current relationship between the ruling circles of the United States and the USSR. These statements are echoed in an even more unrestrained tone by the overwhelming majority of the American press organs. Talk about a "third war ," meaning a war against the Soviet Union, and even a direct call for this war—with the threat of using the atomic bomb—such is the content of the statements on relations with the Soviet Union by reactionaries at public meetings and in the press. At the present time, preaching war against the Soviet Union is not a monopoly of the far-right, yellow American press represented by the newspaper associations of Hearst and McCormick. This anti-Soviet campaign also has been joined by the "reputable" and "respectable" organs of the conservative press, such as the New York Times and New York Herald Tribune. Indicative in this respect are the numerous articles by Walter Lippmann in which he almost undisguisedly calls on the United States to launch a strike against the Soviet Union in the most vulnerable areas of the south and southeast of the USSR.

The basic goal of this anti-Soviet campaign of American "public opinion" is to exert political pressure on the Soviet Union and compel it to make concessions. Another, no less important goal of the campaign is the attempt to create an atmosphere of war psychosis among the masses, who are weary of war, thus making it easier for the U.S. government to carry out measures for the

maintenance of high military potential. It was in this very atmosphere that the law on universal military service in peacetime was
passed by Congress, that the huge military budget was adopted,
and that plans are being worked out for the construction of an
extensive system of naval and air bases.

e) Of course, all of these measures for maintaining a high
military potential are not goals in themselves. They are only
intended to prepare the conditions for winning world supremacy
in a new war, the date for which, to be sure, cannot be determined
now by anyone, but which is contemplated by the most bellicose
circles of American imperialism.

Careful note should be taken of the fact that the preparation
by the United States for a future war is being conducted with the
prospect of war against the Soviet Union, which in the eyes of
American imperialists is the main obstacle in the path of the
United States to world domination. This is indicated by facts such
as the tactical training of the American army for war with the
Soviet Union as the future opponent, the siting of American
strategic bases in regions from which it is possible to launch strikes
on Soviet territory, intensified training and strengthening of
Arctic regions as close approaches to the USSR, and attempts to
prepare Germany and Japan to use those countries in a war
against the USSR.

[signed]
N. Novikov

The Kennan 'Long Telegram'
Moscow, February 22, 1946

Answer to Dept's 284, Feb. 3,[11] involves questions so intricate, so delicate, so strange to our form of thought, and so important to analysis of our international environment that I cannot compress answers into single brief message without yielding to what I feel would be dangerous degree of oversimplification. I hope, therefore, Dept will bear with me if I submit in answer to this question five parts, subjects of which will be roughly as follows:

(1) Basic features of postwar Soviet outlook.

(2) Background of this outlook.

(3) Its projection in practical policy on official level.

(4) Its projection on unofficial level.

(5) Practical deductions from standpoint of US policy.

I apologize in advance for this burdening of telegraphic channel; but questions involved are of such urgent importance, particularly in view of recent events, that our answers to them, if they deserve attention at all, seem to me to deserve it at once. There follows:

Part 1: Basic Features of Postwar Soviet Outlook, as Put Forward by Official Propaganda Machine, Are as Follows

(a) USSR still lives in antagonistic "capitalist encirclement" with which in the long run there can be no permanent peaceful coexistence. As stated by Stalin in 1927 to a delegation of American workers: "In course of further development of international revolution there will emerge two centers of world significance: a socialist center, drawing to itself the countries which tend toward socialism, and a capitalist center, drawing to itself the countries that incline toward capitalism. Battle between these two centers for command of world economy will decide fate of capitalism and of communism in entire world."

(b) Capitalist world is beset with internal conflicts, inherent in nature of capitalist society. These conflicts are insoluble by means of peaceful compromise. Greatest of them is that between England and US.

(c) Internal conflicts of capitalism inevitably generate wars. Wars thus generated may be of two kinds: intra-capitalist wars between two capitalist states and wars of intervention against socialist world. Smart capitalists, vainly seeking escape from inner conflicts of capitalism, incline toward latter.

(d) Intervention against USSR, while it would be disastrous to those who undertook it, would cause renewed delay in progress of Soviet socialism and must therefore be forestalled at all costs.

(e) Conflicts between capitalist states, though likewise fraught with danger for USSR, nevertheless hold out great possibilities for advancement of socialist cause, particularly if USSR remains militarily powerful, ideologically monolithic and faithful to its present brilliant leadership.

(f) It must be borne in mind that capitalist world is not all bad. In addition to hopelessly reactionary and bourgeois elements, it includes (1) certain wholly enlightened and positive elements united in acceptable communistic parties and (2) certain other elements (now described for tactical reasons as progressive or democratic) whose reactions, aspirations and activities happen to be "objectively" favorable to interests of USSR. These last must be encouraged and utilized for Soviet purposes.

(g) Among negative elements of bourgeois-capitalist society, most dangerous of all are those whom Lenin called false friends of the people, namely moderate-socialist or social-democratic leaders (in other words, non-Communist left-wing). These are more dangerous than out-and-out reactionaries, for latter at least march under their true colors, whereas moderate left-wing leaders confuse people by employing devices of socialism to serve interests of reactionary capital.

So much for premises. To what deductions do they lead from standpoint of Soviet policy? To following:

(a) Everything must be done to advance relative strength of USSR as factor in international society. Conversely, no opportunity must be missed to reduce strength and influence, collectively as well as individually, of capitalist powers.

(b) Soviet efforts, and those of Russia's friends abroad, must be directed toward deepening and exploiting of differences and conflicts between capitalist powers. If these eventually deepen into an "imperialist" war, this war must be turned into revolutionary upheavals within the various capitalist countries.

(c) "Democratic-progressive" elements abroad are to be utilized to maximum to bring pressure to bear on capitalist governments along lines agreeable to Soviet interests.

(d) Relentless battle must be waged against socialist and social-democratic leaders abroad.

Part 2: Background of Outlook

Before examining ramifications of this party line in practice there are certain aspects of it to which I wish to draw attention.

First, it does not represent natural outlook of Russian people. Latter are, by and large, friendly to outside world, eager for experience of it, eager to measure against it talents they are conscious of possessing, eager above all to live in peace and enjoy fruits of their own labor. Party line only represents thesis which official propaganda machine puts forward with great skill and persistence to a public often remarkably resistant in the stronghold of its innermost thoughts. But party line is binding for outlook and conduct of people who make up apparatus of power—party, secret police and Government—and it is exclusively with these that we have to deal.

Second, please note that premises on which this party line is based are for most part simply not true. Experience has shown that peaceful and mutually profitable coexistence of capitalist and socialist states is entirely possible. Basic internal conflicts in advanced countries are no longer primarily those arising out of capitalist ownership of means of production, but are ones arising from advanced urbanism and industrialism as such, which Russia has thus far been spared not by socialism but only by her own backwardness. Internal rivalries of capitalism do not always generate wars; and not all wars are attributable to this cause. To speak of possibility of intervention against USSR today, after elimination of Germany and Japan and after example of recent war, is sheerest nonsense. If not provoked by forces of intolerance and subversion, "capitalist" world of today is quite capable of living at peace with itself and with Russia. Finally, no sane person has reason to doubt sincerity of moderate socialist leaders in Western countries. Nor is it fair to deny success of their efforts to improve conditions for working population whenever, as in Scandinavia, they have been given chance to show what they could do.

Falseness of these premises, every one of which predates recent war, was amply demonstrated by that conflict itself. Anglo-American differences did not turn out to be major differences of Western world. Capitalist countries, other than those of Axis, showed no disposition to solve their differences by joining in crusade against USSR. Instead of imperialist war turning into civil wars and revolution, USSR found itself obliged to fight side by side with capitalist powers for an avowed community of aims.

Nevertheless, all these theses, however baseless and disproven, are being boldly put forward again today. What does this indicate? It indicates that Soviet party line is not based on any objective analysis of situation beyond Russia's borders; that it has, indeed, little to do with conditions outside of Russia; that it arises mainly from basic inner-Russian necessities which existed before recent war and exist today.

At bottom of Kremlin's neurotic view of world affairs is traditional and instinctive Russian sense of insecurity. Originally, this was insecurity of a peaceful agricultural people trying to live on vast exposed plain in neighborhood of fierce nomadic peoples. To this was added, as Russia came into contact with economically advanced West, fear of more competent, more powerful, more highly organized societies in that area. But this latter type of insecurity was one which afflicted Russian rulers rather than Russian people; for Russian rulers have invariably sensed that their rule was relatively archaic in form, fragile and artificial in its psychological foundations, unable to stand comparison or contact with political systems of Western countries. For this reason they have always feared foreign penetration, feared direct contact between Western world and their own, feared what would happen if Russians learned truth about world without or if foreigners learned truth about world within. And they have learned to seek security only in patient but deadly struggle for total destruction of rival power, never in compacts and compromises with it.

It was no coincidence that Marxism, which had smouldered ineffectively for half a century in Western Europe, caught hold and blazed for the first time in Russia. Only in this land which had never known a friendly neighbor or indeed any tolerant equilibrium of separate powers, either internal or international, could a doctrine thrive which viewed economic conflicts of society as insoluble by peaceful means. After establishment of Bolshevist regime, Marxist dogma, rendered even more truculent and intolerant by Lenin's interpretation, became a perfect vehicle for sense of insecurity with which Bolsheviks, even more than previous Russian rulers, were afflicted. In this dogma, with its basic altruism of purpose, they found justification for their instinctive fear of outside world, for the dictatorship without which they did not know how to rule, for cruelties they did not dare not to inflict, for sacrifices they felt bound to demand. In the name of Marxism they sacrificed every single ethical value in their methods and tactics. Today they cannot dispense with it. It is fig leaf of their moral and intellectual respectability. Without it they would stand before history, at best, as only the last of that long succession of cruel and wasteful Russian rulers who have relentlessly forced country on to ever new heights of military power in order to guarantee external security of their internally weak regimes. This is why Soviet purposes must always be solemnly clothed in trappings of Marxism, and why no one should underrate importance of dogma in Soviet affairs. Thus Soviet leaders are driven [by] necessities of their own past and present position to put forward a dogma which [apparent omission] outside world as evil, hostile and menacing, but as bearing within itself germs of creeping disease and destined to be wracked with growing internal convulsions until it is given final coup de grace by rising power of socialism and yields to new and better world. This thesis provides justification for that increase of military and police power of Russian state, for that isolation of Russian population from outside world, and for that fluid and constant pressure to extend limits of Russian police power which are together the natural and instinctive urges of Russian rulers. Basically this is only the steady advance of uneasy Russian nationalism, a centuries old movement in which conceptions of offense and defense are inextricably confused. But in new guise of international Marxism, with its honeyed promises to a desperate and war-torn outside world, it is more dangerous and insidious than ever before.

It should not be thought from above that Soviet party line is necessarily disingenuous and insincere on part of all those who put it forward. Many of them are too ignorant of outside world and mentally too dependent to question [apparent omission] self-hypnotism, and who have no difficulty making themselves believe what they find it comforting and convenient to believe. Finally we have the unsolved mystery as to who, if anyone, in this great land actually receives accurate and unbiased information about outside world. In atmosphere of oriental secretiveness and conspiracy which pervades this Government, possibilities for distorting or poisoning sources and currents of information are infinite. The very disrespect of Russians for objective truth—indeed, their disbelief in its existence—leads them to view all stated facts as instruments for furtherance of one ulterior purpose or another. There is good reason to suspect that this Government is actually a conspiracy within a conspiracy; and I for one am reluctant to believe that Stalin himself receives anything like an objective picture of outside world. Here there is ample scope for the type of subtle intrigue at which Russians are past masters. Inability of foreign governments to place their case squarely before Russian policy makers—extent to which they are delivered up in their relations with Russia to good graces of obscure and unknown advisers whom they never see and cannot influence—this to my mind is most disquieting feature of diplomacy in Moscow, and one which Western statesmen would do well to keep in mind if they would understand nature of difficulties encountered here.

Part 3: Projection of Soviet Outlook in Practical Policy on Official Level

We have now seen nature and background of Soviet program. What may we expect by way of its practical implementation?

Soviet policy, as Department implies in its query under reference, is conducted on two planes: (1) official plane represented by actions undertaken officially in name of Soviet Government; and (2) subterranean plane of actions undertaken by agencies for which Soviet Government does not admit responsibility.

Policy promulgated on both planes will be calculated to serve basic policies (a) to (d) outlined in part 1. Actions taken on different planes will differ considerably, but will dovetail into each other in purpose, timing and effect.

On official plane we must look for following:

(a) Internal policy devoted to increasing in every way strength and prestige of Soviet state: intensive military-industrialization; maximum development of armed forces; great displays to impress outsiders; continued secretiveness about internal matters, designed to conceal weaknesses and to keep opponents in the dark.

(b) Wherever it is considered timely and promising, efforts will be made to advance official limits of Soviet power. For the moment, these efforts are restricted to certain neighboring points conceived of here as being of immediate strategic necessity, such as northern Iran, Turkey, possibly Bornholm. However, other points may at any time come into question, if and as concealed Soviet political power is extended to new areas. Thus a "friendly" Persian Government might be asked to grant Russia a port on Persian Gulf. Should Spain fall under Communist control, question of Soviet base at Gibraltar Strait might be activated. But such claims will appear on official level only when unofficial preparation is complete.

(c) Russians will participate officially in international organizations where they see opportunity of extending Soviet power or of inhibiting or diluting power of others. Moscow sees in UNO not the mechanism for a permanent and stable world society founded on mutual interest and aims of all nations, but an arena in which aims just mentioned can be favorably pursued. As long as UNO is considered here to serve this purpose, Soviets will remain with it. But if at any time they come to conclusion that it is serving to embarrass or frustrate their aims for power expansion and if they see better prospects for pursuit of these aims along other lines, they will not hesitate to abandon UNO. This would imply, however, that they felt themselves strong enough to split unity of other nations by their withdrawal, to render UNO ineffective as a threat to their aims or security, and to replace it with an international weapon more effective from their viewpoint. Thus Soviet attitude toward UNO will depend largely on loyalty of other nations to it, and on degree of vigor, decisiveness and cohesion with which these nations defend in UNO the peaceful and hopeful concept of international life, which that organization represents to our way of thinking. I reiterate, Moscow has no abstract devotion to UNO ideals. Its attitude to that organization will remain essentially pragmatic and tactical.

(d) Toward colonial areas and backward or dependent peoples, Soviet policy, even on official plane, will be directed toward weakening of power and influence and contacts of advanced Western nations, on theory that insofar as this policy is successful, there will be created a vacuum which will favor Communist-Soviet penetration. Soviet pressure for participation in trusteeship arrangements thus represents, in my opinion, a desire to be in a position to complicate and inhibit exertion of Western influence at such points rather than to provide major channel for exerting of Soviet power. Latter motive is not lacking, but for this Soviets prefer to rely on other channels than official trusteeship arrangements. Thus we may expect to find Soviets asking for admission everywhere to trusteeship or similar arrangements and using levers thus acquired to weaken Western influence among such peoples.

(e) Russians will strive energetically to develop Soviet representation in, and official ties with, countries in which they sense strong possibilities of opposition to Western centers of power. This applies to such widely separated points as Germany, Argentina, Middle Eastern countries, etc.

(f) In international economic matters, Soviet policy will really be dominated by pursuit of autarchy for Soviet Union and Soviet-dominated adjacent areas taken together. That, however, will be underlying policy. As far as official line is concerned, position is not yet clear. Soviet Government has shown strange reticence since termination hostilities on subject foreign trade. If large-scale long-term credits should be forthcoming, I believe Soviet Government may eventually again do lip service, as it did in 1930's, to desirability of building up international economic exchanges in general. Otherwise I think it possible Soviet foreign trade may be restricted largely to Soviet's own security sphere, including occupied areas in

Germany, and that a cold official shoulder may be turned to principle of general economic collaboration among nations.

(g) With respect to cultural collaboration, lip service will likewise be rendered to desirability of deepening cultural contacts between peoples, but this will not in practice be interpreted in any way which could weaken security position of Soviet peoples. Actual manifestations of Soviet policy in this respect will be restricted to arid channels of closely shepherded official visits and functions, with superabundance of vodka and speeches and dearth of permanent effects.

(h) Beyond this, Soviet official relations will take what might be called "correct" course with individual foreign governments, with great stress being laid on prestige of Soviet Union and its representatives and with punctilious attention to protocol, as distinct from good manners.

Part 4: Following May Be Said as to What We May Expect by Way of Implementation of Basic Soviet Policies on Unofficial, or Subterranean Plane, i.e., on Plane for Which Soviet Government Accepts No Responsibility

Agencies utilized for promulgation of policies on this plane are following:

1. Inner central core of Communist parties in other countries. While many of persons who compose this category may also appear and act in unrelated public capacities, they are in reality working closely together as an underground operating directorate of world communism, a concealed Comintern[12] tightly coordinated and directed by Moscow. It is important to remember that this inner core is actually working on underground lines, despite legality of parties with which it is associated.

2. Rank and file of Communist parties. Note distinction is drawn between these and persons defined in paragraph 1. This distinction has become much sharper in recent years. Whereas formerly foreign Communist parties represented a curious (and from Moscow's standpoint often inconvenient) mixture of conspiracy and legitimate activity, now the conspiratorial element has been neatly concentrated in inner circle and ordered underground, while rank and file—no longer even taken into

confidence about realities of movement—are thrust forward as bona fide internal partisans of certain political tendencies within their respective countries, genuinely innocent of conspiratorial connection with foreign states. Only in certain countries where communists are numerically strong do they now regularly appear and act as a body. As a rule they are used to penetrate, and to influence or dominate, as case may be, other organizations less likely to be suspected of being tools of Soviet Government, with a view to accomplishing their purposes through [apparent omission] organizations, rather than by direct action as a separate political party.

3. A wide variety of national associations or bodies which can be dominated or influenced by such penetration. These include: labor unions, youth leagues, women's organizations, racial societies, religious societies, social organizations, cultural groups, liberal magazines, publishing houses, etc.

4. International organizations which can be similarly penetrated through influence over various national components. Labor, youth and women's organizations are prominent among them. Particular, almost vital, importance is attached in this connection to international labor movement. In this, Moscow sees possibility of sidetracking Western governments in world affairs and building up international lobby capable of compelling governments to take actions favorable to Soviet interests in various countries and of paralyzing actions disagreeable to USSR.

5. Russian Orthodox Church, with its foreign branches, and through it the Eastern Orthodox Church in general.

6. Pan-Slav movement and other movements (Azerbaijan, Armenian, Turcoman, etc.) based on racial groups within Soviet Union.

7. Governments or governing groups willing to lend themselves to Soviet purposes in one degree or another, such as present Bulgarian and Yugoslav governments, North Persian regime, Chinese Communists, etc. Not only propaganda machines but actual policies of these regimes can be placed extensively at disposal of USSR.

It may be expected that component parts of this far-flung apparatus will be utilized, in accordance with their individual suitability, as follows:

(a) To undermine general political and strategic potential of major Western Powers. Efforts will be made in such countries to disrupt national self-confidence, to hamstring measures of national defense, to increase social and industrial unrest, to stimulate all forms of disunity. All persons with grievances, whether economic or racial, will be urged to seek redress not in mediation and compromise, but in defiant, violent struggle for destruction of other elements of society. Here poor will be set against rich, black against white, young against old, newcomers against established residents, etc.

(b) On unofficial plane particularly violent efforts will be made to weaken power and influence of Western Powers [on] colonial, backward, or dependent peoples. On this level, no holds will be barred. Mistakes and weaknesses of Western colonial administration will be mercilessly exposed and exploited. Liberal opinion in Western countries will be mobilized to weaken colonial policies. Resentment among dependent peoples will be stimulated. And while latter are being encouraged to seek independence [from] Western Powers, Soviet dominated puppet political machines will be undergoing preparation to take over domestic power in respective colonial areas when independence is achieved.

(c) Where individual governments stand in path of Soviet purposes pressure will be brought for their removal from office. This can happen where governments directly oppose Soviet foreign policy aims (Turkey, Iran), where they seal their territories off against Communist penetration (Switzerland, Portugal), or where they compete too strongly (like Labor Government in England) for moral domination among elements which it is important for Communists to dominate. (Sometimes, two of these elements are present in a single case. Then Communist opposition becomes particularly shrill and savage.)

(d) In foreign countries Communists will, as a rule, work toward destruction of all forms of personal independence—economic, political or moral. Their system can handle only individuals who have been brought into complete dependence on higher power. Thus, persons who are financially independent—such as individual businessmen, estate owners, successful farmers, artisans—and all those who exercise local leadership or have local prestige—such as popular local clergymen or political figures—are anathema. It is not by chance that even in USSR local officials are kept constantly on move from one job to another, to prevent their taking root.

(e) Everything possible will be done to set major Western Powers against each other. Anti-British talk will be plugged among Americans, anti-American talk among British. Continentals, including Germans, will be taught to abhor both Anglo-Saxon powers. Where suspicions exist, they will be fanned; where not, ignited. No effort will be spared to discredit and combat all efforts which threaten to lead to any sort of unity or cohesion among other [apparent omission] from which Russia might be excluded. Thus, all forms of international organization not amenable to Communist penetration and control, whether it be the Catholic [apparent omission] international economic concerns, or the international fraternity of royalty and aristocracy, must expect to find themselves under fire from many, and often [apparent omission].

(f) In general, all Soviet efforts on unofficial international plane will be negative and destructive in character, designed to tear down sources of strength beyond reach of Soviet control. This is only in line with basic Soviet instinct that there can be no compromise with rival power and that constructive work can start only when Communist power is dominant. But behind all this will be applied insistent, unceasing pressure for penetration and command of key positions in administration and especially in police apparatus of foreign countries. The Soviet regime is a police regime par excellence, reared in the dim half world of Tsarist police intrigue, accustomed to think primarily in terms of police power. This should never be lost sight of in gauging Soviet motives.

Part 5: [Practical Deductions from Standpoint of US Policy]

In summary, we have here a political force committed fanatically to the belief that with US there can be no permanent modus vivendi, that it is desirable and necessary that the internal harmony of our society be disrupted, our traditional way of life be destroyed, the international authority of our state be broken, if Soviet power is to be secure. This political force has complete power of disposition over energies of one of world's greatest peoples and resources of world's richest national territory, and is borne along by deep and powerful currents of Russian nationalism. In addition, it has an elaborate and far-flung apparatus for exertion of its influence in other countries, an apparatus of amazing flexibility and versatility, managed by people whose experience and skill in underground methods are presumably without parallel in history. Finally, it is seemingly inaccessible to considerations of reality in its basic reactions. For it, the vast fund of objective fact about human society is not, as with us, the measure against which outlook is constantly being tested and re-formed, but a grab bag from which individual items are selected arbitrarily and tendenciously to bolster an outlook already preconceived. This is admittedly not a pleasant picture. Problem of how to cope with this force [is] undoubtedly greatest task our diplomacy has ever faced and probably greatest it will ever have to face. It should be point of departure from which our political general staff work at present juncture should proceed. It should be approached with same thoroughness and care as solution of major strategic problem in war and, if necessary, with no smaller outlay in planning effort. I cannot attempt to suggest all answers here. But I would like to record my conviction that problem is within our power to solve—and that without recourse to any general military conflict. And in support of this conviction there are certain observations of a more encouraging nature I should like to make:

(1) Soviet power, unlike that of Hitlerite Germany, is neither schematic nor adventuristic. It does not work by fixed plans. It does not take unnecessary risks. Impervious to logic of reason, and it is highly sensitive to logic of force. For this reason it can easily withdraw—and usually does—when strong resistance is encountered at any point. Thus, if the adversary has sufficient force and makes clear his readiness to use it, he rarely has to do so. If situations are properly handled there need be no prestige-engaging showdowns.

(2) Gauged against Western world as a whole, Soviets are still by far the weaker force. Thus, their success will really depend on degree of cohesion, firmness and vigor which Western world can muster. And this is factor which it is within our power to influence.

(3) Success of Soviet system, as form of internal power, is not yet finally proven. It has yet to be demonstrated that it can survive

supreme test of successive transfer of power from one individual or group to another. Lenin's death was first such transfer, and its effects wracked Soviet state for 15 years. After Stalin's death or retirement will be second. But even this will not be final test. Soviet internal system will now be subjected, by virtue of recent territorial expansions, to series of additional strains which once proved severe tax on Tsardom. We here are convinced that never since termination of civil war have mass of Russian people been emotionally farther removed from doctrines of Communist Party than they are today. In Russia, party has now become a great and—for the moment—highly successful apparatus of dictatorial administration, but it has ceased to be a source of emotional inspiration. Thus, internal soundness and permanence of movement need not yet be regarded as assured.

(4) All Soviet propaganda beyond Soviet security sphere is basically negative and destructive. It should therefore be relatively easy to combat it by any intelligent and really constructive program.

For these reasons I think we may approach calmly and with good heart problem of how to deal with Russia. As to how this approach should be made, I only wish to advance, by way of conclusion, following comments:

(1) Our first step must be to apprehend, and recognize for what it is, the nature of the movement with which we are dealing. We must study it with same courage, detachment, objectivity, and same determination not to be emotionally provoked or unseated by it, with which doctor studies unruly and unreasonable individual.

(2) We must see that our public is educated to realities of Russian situation. I cannot overemphasize importance of this. Press cannot do this alone. It must be done mainly by Government, which is necessarily more experienced and better informed on practical problems involved. In this we need not be deterred by [ugliness?] of picture. I am convinced that there would be far less hysterical anti-Sovietism in our country today if realities of this situation were better understood by our people. There is nothing as dangerous or as terrifying as the unknown. It may also be argued that to reveal more information on our difficulties with Russia would reflect unfavorably on Russian-American relations. I feel that if there is any real risk here involved, it is one which we

should have courage to face, and sooner the better. But I cannot see what we would be risking. Our stake in this country, even coming on heels of tremendous demonstrations of our friendship for Russian people, is remarkably small. We have here no investments to guard, no actual trade to lose, virtually no citizens to protect, few cultural contacts to preserve. Our only stake lies in what we hope rather than what we have; and I am convinced we have better chance of realizing those hopes if our public is enlightened and if our dealings with Russians are placed entirely on realistic and matter-of-fact basis.

(3) Much depends on health and vigor of our own society. World communism is like malignant parasite which feeds only on diseased tissue. This is point at which domestic and foreign policies meet. Every courageous and incisive measure to solve internal problems of our own society, to improve self-confidence, discipline, morale and community spirit of our own people, is a diplomatic victory over Moscow worth a thousand diplomatic notes and joint communiqués. If we cannot abandon fatalism and indifference in face of deficiencies of our own society, Moscow will profit—Moscow cannot help profiting by them in its foreign policies.

(4) We must formulate and put forward for other nations a much more positive and constructive picture of sort of world we would like to see than we have put forward in past. It is not enough to urge people to develop political processes similar to our own. Many foreign peoples, in Europe at least, are tired and frightened by experiences of past, and are less interested in abstract freedom than in security. They are seeking guidance rather than responsibilities. We should be better able than Russians to give them this. And, unless we do, Russians certainly will.

(5) Finally we must have courage and self-confidence to cling to our own methods and conceptions of human society. After all, the greatest danger that can befall us in coping with this problem of Soviet communism is that we shall allow ourselves to become like those with whom we are coping.

KENNAN

The Roberts Cables

Moscow, March 14, 1946, Section 1

In my despatch No. 799 of October 31st I attempted to review Soviet policy and the state of Anglo-Soviet relations after the breakdown of the Council of Foreign Ministers in London. The outlook was not then entirely encouraging, and there were clearly many danger signs ahead. But Mr. Molotov, making in place of Generalissimo Stalin what is the most important annual statement of Soviet policy, gave on November 6th a relatively reassuring picture of Soviet aims and in particular committed the Soviet Union to continued international cooperation within the United Nations Organisation, and more particularly within the framework of the Big Three. The sober hopes fostered by this statement have not, however, been borne out in succeeding months, and the time now seems overdue to review the position once again after the visit paid by you and Mr. Byrnes to Moscow and the meeting of the General Assembly in London, to attempt once again to assess Soviet policy in what has been described here as the period of peaceful reconstruction ahead, and even to consider on what basis the Anglo-Soviet Alliance, which made so essential a contribution to the victory of the United Nations, can do useful service in the peace.

2. The more or less simultaneous departure from Moscow of the British, American and French Ambassadors marks a new epoch in the relations of the Soviet Union with the outside world. These changes have taken place at a time when there is more anxious questioning concerning the present behaviour and

ultimate intentions of the Soviet Union than at any period since the collapse of foreign intervention. This anxiety is by no means confined to circles normally suspicious of the Soviet Union, and has been stated frankly and authoritatively in your own speech of February 21st in the House of Commons, and subsequently by Mr. Byrnes, Mr. Vandenberg and also by Mr. Winston Churchill in the United States. Generalissimo Stalin's reply today to Mr. Churchill, following upon a growing anti-British press campaign and coupled with the mounting tension in Persia, has brought matters to a head.

3. When Mr. Molotov spoke on November 6th a deadlock existed as regards Soviet relations with her two major allies in the Far East and also in the Balkans. This prevented any progress with the signing of peace treaties even with Italy and the minor satellites. The shadow of the atom bomb darkened our relations and behind every manifestation of Anglo-American solidarity, e.g., in Bulgaria or Roumania, the rulers of the Soviet Union, until then confident of the overwhelming strength of the Red Army, saw the menace of an Anglo-American bloc, possessing this decisive weapon and therefore capable not only of depriving the Soviet Union of the fruits of the victories of the Red Army but even of endangering the security which the Soviet Union had so hardly won. The Soviet Government seemed to feel that in such an atmosphere they could make no concessions, and indeed they soon began to counterattack against Britain as the weaker member of what they regarded as an Anglo-American combination. Already existing difficulties in Greece, Persia and the Middle East generally, and over the so-called "Western bloc" and the administration of Germany, were intensified. A warning note was sounded for the first time since the war in Soviet propaganda in regard to such questions as India, Egypt and colonies in South-East Asia, issues on which the Soviet press had long been silent. Above all, increasing attention was devoted to the renewed Marxist-Leninist ideological campaign. Britain as the home of capitalism, imperialism and now of social democracy is a main target and is shown up as the centre of opposition to the progressive ideas and forces of which the Soviet Union claims to be the chief patron.

4. In this atmosphere, which clearly compromised the chances of satisfactorily launching the UNO, it is not surprising that the

United States administration took fright. Mr. Byrnes therefore took the initiative in breaking the existing deadlock and proposed the meeting of foreign ministers, which took place in Moscow in December. You yourself had serious doubts, which were also felt by many foreign observers in Moscow, of the wisdom of this step. The tough and hard-headed men in the Kremlin had certainly been counting upon it, since they were confident that their own nerves were stronger than those of the Western democracies and that they could therefore rely upon one or another of the latter to make concessions of form and of substance in order to restore harmony with the Soviet Union.

5. I need not review at any length the results of the Moscow meeting. These were favourable to the Soviet Union insofar as she achieved her aims over the recognition by America and Britain of the Roumanian and (as it then seemed) the Bulgarian governments and over the principles upon which the foreign ministers should resume work on the drafting of peace treaties with the European satellites. Arrangements acceptable to the Soviet Government were also made in respect of Far Eastern questions in general and of the procedure for dealing with the problem of atomic energy in the UNO. The Americans also achieved, or seemed at the time to have achieved, their main objectives. Such small advantages as His Majesty's Government may have derived from the meeting, apart from the general advantage of breaking the deadlock and providing a better atmosphere for the London meeting of the General Assembly, were more than outweighed by the lack of any agreement on Persia and the continued stubbornness of the Soviet attitude on Turkey. These urgent questions were, despite all your efforts, left in suspense, and, as I endeavoured to show in my despatch No. 30 of January 16th, we were left to face with doubtful American backing constantly increasing Soviet pressure in the whole zone vital to British security between India and the Dardanelles. The Moscow meeting did, however, enable you to review with Generalissimo Stalin and Mr. Molotov the general state of Anglo-Soviet relations and to show them very clearly not only our progressive aims in regard to the semi-dependent peoples of India, the Middle East and the colonial empire, but also to explain clearly what we regarded as our vital interests, for example, in regard to the continued independence and integrity of Turkey, and that there was a limit

beyond which we could not tolerate continued Soviet infiltration and undermining of our position.

6. The absence of Mr. Molotov from the UNO meeting in London and the long delay in Mr. Vyshinski's arrival there were not promising auguries for the Soviet attitude in London. Vyshinski began by successfully shelving the Persian appeal, and followed this up with heavy counterattacks upon British policy in Greece, Indonesia, the Levant, and finally in respect of the Anders army in Italy. The meetings of the Security Council in London thus became, owing to deliberate Soviet action, a forum for public Anglo-Soviet dispute, and when the first session of the General Assembly broke up and the Security Council adjourned, there was little to show that the Soviet Union still regarded Britain under a Labour Government as an ally, or even a friend. Most disturbing of all, we gained no credit with the Soviet Government for our repeated attempts at conciliation, e.g., our endeavour to prevent the Persian question coming before the UNO, and our final compromise to save Soviet "face" over Greece. These, like our earlier concessions in regard to Poland, Yugoslavia, Roumania and Bulgaria, only served to sharpen the next Soviet attack.

7. Outside the UNO the Soviet Ambassador in Greece has brazenly suggested that the Soviet Union should be given a base in the Dodecanese. In Persia, a pro-Soviet prime minister was found and brought to Moscow in the hope that he could be persuaded to cover the achievement of Russian aims with a decent cloak of Soviet-Persian agreement. The constant press campaign against alleged British actions in Persia was whipped up. In regard to Turkey, concurrently with continued publicity for Armenian and Georgian territorial claims, the Soviet Ambassador resumed contact with the Turkish Government, in order to persuade them that they should abandon the British connexion and come to terms directly with the Soviet Government. The Kurds are being openly encouraged by Soviet agents and have already set up in Persian Azerbaijan the semblance of an autonomous state. Propaganda against our position in Egypt and the Arab world generally, in India and our colonies in the Far East, has become a main feature of the Soviet press and wireless. "National liberation movements" are being encouraged against us in much the same way as national liberation movements against Germany were fostered during the war by the Soviet Union. In Europe Allied military administration

of Trieste continues to be the subject of constant criticism. A major propaganda campaign has been opened to suggest that the Anders army, under our command, is plotting to restore fascism in Poland and throughout Europe. In Poland itself a campaign has been opened to discredit M. Mikolajczyk and to remove him from office, while every effort is also being made to hamper good Anglo-Polish relations. In Yugoslavia also our influence is being consistently weakened. Hungary and Austria, which voted for moderate parties in the recent elections, are now being subjected to strong political and economic pressure from the Soviet Union to teach them a lesson. In Italy, and above all in France, the Communist parties are being encouraged, and communist propaganda is constantly directed against us. More recently developments in regard to Spain have given the Russians their opportunity to show their continued interest in that country, where they are prepared to encourage a new civil war regardless of British interests. Most serious of all, Anglo-Soviet differences are also coming to a head in Germany itself, where the Russians, not content with achieving a joint Communist–Social-Democratic bloc in Berlin and with a rising campaign of criticism of the administration of our zone of Germany, are now encouraging the Communists to advocate a united "democratic" Germany in full control of the Ruhr. This in itself suggests that Soviet hostility to the so-called Western bloc is as strong as ever, and indeed Mr. Vyshinski has recently admitted as much to M. Spaak, to whom he accused us of building up such a bloc (to include Poland and Czechoslovakia) against the Soviet Union.

8. This is a sombre picture, and it is hardly surprising that we ask ourselves what lies behind these manifestations of Soviet opposition to a Britain which has for the past four and a half years constantly endeavoured, not only to support the Soviet war effort—often at the expense of our own—but also to meet Soviet territorial and other requirements even though in some cases, as Poland, we had grave doubts whether these requirements, taken as a whole, were legitimate or opportune. It is possible that our very forbearance and cooperative spirit have been misinterpreted as weakness here. Indeed, a diplomatic colleague recently told me that an intelligent Soviet acquaintance of his had informed him that Britain was now the sick man of Europe, much as Turkey had been throughout the 19th century, and that our fate during the

coming years was likely to resemble that of the Austro-Hungarian Empire. Certainly the present line of Soviet policy and propaganda, and the viciousness of Soviet attacks upon our interests throughout the world, lend some colour to this hypothesis. But I am not convinced that present Soviet policy towards us is in fact based upon a conviction of our weakness. On the contrary, the very vehemence of Soviet criticism and the almost hysterical manner in which we are being attacked at all points at once suggest a certain fear of our inherent strength, which may have been increased by the recent London meeting of the UNO at which the Soviet delegates found the whole world, with few exceptions, ranged on our side under your own moral leadership. The rulers of Russia already realised when Labour was returned to power at the general election last July that there was now a progressive force in the world of equal and possibly greater attraction than their own communist system. They also know, despite all attempts to divide us, that behind Britain stand in the last resort not only the Dominions but probably also the United States, for whose material strength there is the most pronounced respect here. My impression is therefore that the present Soviet push on all diplomatic fronts simultaneously is partly an attempt to profit from the present fluid state of postwar Europe and the world and from immediate postwar difficulties, but partly also an almost desperate effort to seize advanced positions and to dig in before the inevitable reaction against high-handed Soviet actions sets in with a return to more normal and peaceful conditions. This applies in particular to Europe, Persia and Turkey. In India, in the rest of the Middle East and in the colonies, the Soviet Union no doubt feels greater confidence in the ultimate strength and attraction of its ideas, as I have suggested in my despatch No. 30, and it is therefore in those areas that we are likely to experience more intense and constant Soviet pressure.

9. My feeling that there may be a touch of desperation behind much of present-day Soviet policy is strengthened by their recent attitude towards America. The obvious goal of Soviet policy, shown very clearly in the reactions to Mr. Churchill's Fulton speech, must be to keep us and America apart as far as possible, and in this they were not unsuccessful in Moscow last December. But their very lack of moderation since then, the way in which they have pressed their demands simultaneously throughout the

world, the impression they have created that there is no limit to Soviet aims and that a concession in one place merely leads to further demands elsewhere—now seem to have alarmed the Americans as much as ourselves. Above all Soviet behaviour and unilateral actions in the Far East and particularly in Manchuria have extended this alarm to the Chinese and touched the Americans upon a very tender spot. Further and apparently quite unnecessary provocation has been afforded by the recent Soviet flirtation with Colonel Peron's regime in Argentina and by a more active Soviet interest throughout Latin America. Nor has the Soviet Union adopted a helpful attitude towards the United States Government in regard to issues such as Bretton Woods and the proposed conference on international trade and tariffs, to which the American administration attribute such importance. American disquiet can only have been increased by the revelations of Soviet espionage in Canada—a question clearly of direct interest to the United States and affecting their treasured possession of the secret of atomic energy. To complete the picture the Soviet Government have flagrantly broken their treaty obligations in Persia with no attempt to explain themselves and are conducting a most disturbing policy towards Turkey as well. In most of these cases the Soviet Government have handled awkward issues with the greatest possible clumsiness and in a way which can only increase suspicion of their motives.

10. These international events must also be judged against the background of internal developments in the Soviet Union. Last October I reported that there were certain signs of strain and stress, although I suggested that these should not be exaggerated. During the past four months, the Soviet Government have kept the position well under control. The major factors have been the election campaign, which has just concluded with the expected overwhelming vote of confidence in the Communist party and the present Soviet administration, and the preparation of the new Five-Year Plan for the restoration of war damage and the further development of the Soviet economy. I have reported elsewhere upon both these issues. The importance of the Five-Year Plan for our present purposes lies in the emphasis laid upon increasing the economic and military strength of the Soviet Union by maintaining the necessary armaments industry and developing heavy industry. The election campaign enabled the authorities to revive

popular energies and enthusiasm after a certain postwar lassitude and to harness them again to the great tasks ahead. The campaign also included a tremendous revival of orthodox Marxist ideology, which left the impression that the Soviet peoples were a chosen people, and that they were surrounded by a hostile world composed largely of reactionary capitalists and their willing tools in the social democratic movement. Among the developments which have strengthened the Soviet State have been improved labour discipline, the restoration of better discipline in the Red Army, the continued absorption of demobilised men into industry and agriculture, the control—at least in Moscow—of hooliganism, a progressive lowering in prices and a gradual increase in available consumer goods. The Soviet people have also been promised the early abolition of rationing. Finally, a great reorganisation is taking place in the commissariats responsible for the armed forces, industrial production, building and agriculture. This is clearly designed to increase the efficiency and the potential military strength of the Soviet State. So far as the home front is concerned, the Soviet rulers can therefore continue to feel confident that they can conduct their foreign policy with the certainty that it will be accepted by the Soviet public and that the necessary efforts and sacrifices will be made to maintain and increase Soviet military and economic might. On the other hand, they know better than anyone the many serious weaknesses in the present state of the Soviet economy, and Stalin himself has publicly declared that the Soviet Union still needs three or more Five-Year Plans before she can overtake and surpass the achievements of the greatest capitalist states.

11. The present state of Soviet relations with the outside world, and more particularly with Britain, is very different from what we had hoped for on the morrow of our joint victory, and after we have made so many concessions to meet Soviet security requirements. Instead of the Soviet Union gradually settling down to a more normal and friendly relationship with its allies, we are faced with a Soviet policy designed to advance Soviet interests at every possible opportunity, regardless of those of its allies, and it now seems regardless even of treaty obligations. Instead of telling a weary and sorely tried population that, the fascist menace having now been removed, the peoples of the Soviet Union can settle down in peace to work for the improvement of their standards of

living, Soviet propaganda is actively instilling suspicions and distrust of the outside world, of which the Soviet public is being kept in complete ignorance. In recent telegrams I have endeavoured to explain the ever-increasing emphasis laid here upon Marxist-Leninist ideology as the basis for Soviet internal and foreign policy and to show the abnormality of the Soviet Government in its dealings with other governments. The bonds forged by common interests in the war against Germany and Japan are now so visibly parting that the question must be asked whether the Soviet Government still attribute importance to continued cooperation among the Big Three, to the Anglo-Soviet Alliance, and even to the UNO except insofar as this provides a convenient machinery for advancing Soviet interests. In view of the contents of the election speeches by the Soviet leaders which laid down policy in the months ahead, it may even be asked whether the world is not now faced with the danger of a modern equivalent of the religious wars of the 16th century, in which Soviet communism will struggle with Western social democracy and the American version of capitalism for domination of the world. Turning to more immediate and concrete issues, and having regard to the latest developments in Persia, we may even ask ourselves whether the Soviet rulers are not preparing some military adventure in the spring—for example, against Turkey. At times it might seem that Soviet successes have gone to the heads of the Politburo, that they feel that everything is possible and that they can advance their designs throughout the world without fear of serious opposition; or there may simply be a great sense of urgency to achieve as much as possible before resistance becomes too strong. In other words, it is not yet clear how far present Soviet actions and statements are purely tactical and how far they represent the first steps in a carefully considered long-term offensive strategy. When such questions are asked, there is clearly a danger that we may swing from the extreme of optimism about the future of Anglo-Soviet relations, cherished during the war, to the opposite extreme of pessimism in which the Anglo-Soviet Treaty would appear a mere dead letter. In order to form a balanced view of Soviet policy and of the future of Anglo-Soviet relations, this therefore seems a suitable moment to face the realities of the situation and to consider, as I shall endeavour to do in a separate despatch which will reach you shortly, the essential factors in

Soviet thinking and in the Russian national traditions which mould Soviet policy today.

I am sending a copy of this despatch to Washington.

I have the honour to be, with the highest respect,
Sir,
Your most obedient, humble Servant.

[signed]
Frank K. Roberts
Chargé d'Affaires

Moscow, March 17, 1946, Section 2

I undertook in my despatch No. 181 to endeavour to assess the main factors bearing upon Soviet policy and to estimate their effect upon Anglo-Soviet relations in the postwar world. I am only too well aware of the magnitude of the problem and of the difficulties of treating it thoroughly and objectively. I feel, however, that it must now be faced, although I submit the following review with the greatest diffidence and in full consciousness of its inadequacies and shortcomings.

2. There is one fundamental factor affecting Soviet policy dating back to the small beginnings of the Muscovite State. This is the constant striving for security of a State with no natural frontiers and surrounded by enemies. In this all-important respect the rulers and people of Russia are united by a common fear, deeply rooted in Russian history. National security is, in fact, at the bottom of Soviet, as of Imperial Russian, policy, and explains much of the high-handed behaviour of the Kremlin and many of the suspicions genuinely held there concerning the outside world. Russia has always been a more backward State than her neighbours. Even today the Soviet Union, despite its prestige in the world, is more backward than not only Britain or the United States, but than most other European countries. She has grown around a small principality in Moscow, with no natural frontiers and always surrounded by unfriendly neighbours—Tartars, Poles, Turks, Teutonic Knights and Swedes. At the very birth of the new Soviet State the whole world again seemed united against her, and the fears aroused by foreign intervention after 1917 cannot yet have been eradicated from the minds of the rulers of Russia, any more than the fear of communism has been eradicated from that of Western leaders, who nevertheless cooperated with the Soviet Union during the war. The frontiers of Russia have never been fixed and have gone backwards and forwards with defeats or victories in war. But even after her greatest victories in the past Russia has somehow found herself deprived of many of the fruits of those victories, and has never achieved the security which she thought her due reward. Despite this, over the centuries Russia has expanded, as much by peaceful colonisation (e.g., in

Siberia) and by agreement with local leaders (e.g., in Georgia) as by actual conquest.

3. Russia's relations with Britain, which opened on a friendly footing in the mid-sixteenth century, grew steadily in scope and political importance from Peter the Great's reign onwards as Russia expanded towards areas in which Britain herself was closely interested. But wherever British and Russian political interests touched they seemed inevitably to come into conflict, if only because Russia was usually to be found upsetting a state of affairs which Britain regarded as tolerably satisfactory. The result was that Russia and Britain found themselves on opposite sides in the Baltic, in the Near East (where they struggled over the weakening Turkish Empire and over the passages from the Black Sea to the Mediterranean), in Persia and later in the Far East. But in the greatest crises of modern history Britain and Russia have had to turn to each other for support and have found themselves in the same camp. Ivan the Terrible, painfully building up the Russian State against strong foreign and internal enemies, made the first Russian treaty with Britain in order that British ships could bring in supplies by sea. Peter the Great also looked to Britain and Holland for help in building up the Russian navy and Russian economy. In the great crisis of the Napoleonic wars, despite many misunderstandings and clashes of interest between the two countries, Britain and Russia were again together, and between them they saved Europe from French domination. After the Treaty of Vienna and throughout the 19th century relations were strained. The Tsarist system was regarded with the same ideological aversion as the present Communist tyranny, and Alexander I and Nicholas I were feared as Stalin is today. On the other side the Russians distrusted Britain as the home of dangerous liberal ideas which, if they spread abroad, would lead to revolution and disorder. There were constant and serious clashes of interest throughout the Middle East and in South-Eastern Europe, which often threatened war but only once actually led to it. Towards the end of the century there was a fear of Russian strength and of Russian designs on India and the empire which was quite as strong and deep-seated as the anxieties concerning Russian intentions which are now spreading in the Western world. But despite all this, British and Russian interests were reconciled in the 1907 agreement (although this was reached when

Russia was weak after her defeat by Japan and when she was a prey to internal troubles) and once again we found ourselves fighting together against Germany in 1914. Despite all the bitterness left on both sides by the Revolution and foreign intervention, Hitler brought us together again in 1941 and the alliance of 1942 led to our joint victory with the United States in 1945.

4. But until 1945 Britain and Russia were never left face to face. Their relations were conditioned by the coexistence of a strong France, of Prussia and later a powerful German Empire, of Austria-Hungary and even of the Turkish Empire. And, as I have already suggested, in all the greatest European crises since the French Revolution, Britain and Russia were brought together to fight against the domination of Europe by another Great Power, whether France or Germany. Now all that has changed. France is no longer a Great Power. Germany is at all events for the time being of no account. Austria-Hungary and the Turkish Empire no longer exist. The only other world Power is the United States, and there is clearly no reason why Britain and Russia should be brought to combine against her as a menace to their interests or to the peace of the world. Therefore Britain and Russia are now in immediate contact as never before, with no other Power to unite them in self-defence or act as a buffer between them. And between them there is now a greater ideological gulf than even in the 19th century. Instead of the old balance of forces there now exist the UNO and the Big Three, which are in the Soviet view at least closely interconnected. The Soviet Government has always seen the UNO as a body which can only work so long as the Big Three are in agreement or can harmonise their interests behind the scenes. The course of events at the UNO meeting in London, which may well be repeated in New York, has shown that when Big Three cooperation breaks down the UNO itself is at once in danger and that the Soviet Union may then only regard it as a convenient forum in which to embarrass us and to appeal for the support of some among the smaller nations. As after the treaties of Vienna and Versailles, Anglo-Russian relations, with no common enemy to draw us together, are proving fragile and are not contributing to the promotion of closer international organisation.

5. In this new situation, what is the Soviet attitude towards the outside world in general and Britain in particular? This is shown in the ideological line laid down for the Soviet public by

the Communist party, since this not only conditions the thinking of the Soviet public but also guides the activities of the Communist parties throughout the world. This party teaching is not encouraging for the future of Anglo-Soviet cooperation. The tone of party propaganda, and more particularly in the more thoughtful and authoritative publications such as *Bolshevik, World Economy and Peace* and *Party Organisation,* is not only critical of but hostile to the outside world. The great bulk of the information allowed to reach the Soviet public about Britain or the United States is critical or contemptuous. News items are weighted and selected in order to convey the desired impression of a civilisation inferior to that of the Soviet Union and containing within itself the seeds of its own destruction. The United States is painted as a land torn with strikes, with an acute Negro problem, and with the working classes exploited by selfish capitalists. Britain is shown as weakened by the war; the necessary reforms are not being put in hand with enough resolution; the Labour Government is disappointing its supporters and acting as a tool of sinister influences, while fascists are allowed full freedom to conduct their notorious activities. The picture is, of course, even blacker throughout the colonial empire, and in India and the Middle East, where we are found guilty of the sins not only of exploitation but of inefficient leadership.

6. But the Western democracies, weak and disunited though they may be, are shown as the main dangers in a continued capitalist encirclement of the Soviet Union. In this respect, Soviet propaganda and official pronouncements have harked back to the old Soviet attitude of the twenties and early thirties, and now that the German and Japanese menace has been removed, the former allies of the Soviet Union are represented as potential, if not actual, enemies. The capitalist world is, however, shown as profoundly divided both between States and within individual States. In fact, in the orthodox Marxist view, these capitalist States are bound to quarrel amongst themselves, more particularly over control of dwindling raw materials and over colonial territories still existing in the world. The Soviet Union would not be interested in such quarrels within a decaying civilisation were it not for the fact that even the Soviet Union is a member of world society and may be affected by such death struggles within the capitalist world. Above all there is the danger that some leaders of capitalist society

might unite their countries in an attack upon the Soviet Union, if only to distract attention from their own internal problems. The Soviet Union must therefore be constantly on her guard, surrounded as she is by enemies. She must build up her industrial potential to the greatest possible extent and maintain a strong military establishment, even in time of peace. She must improve such backward arms as her air force and navy, and, above all, catch up with the Western democracies over the harnessing of atomic energy.

7. The picture might be less black and the prospects less gloomy if the Soviet Union were prepared to isolate herself completely from the infectious outside world. But this is not likely because, in the hostile capitalist world, there are many good elements such as the Communist party, fellow travellers and liberal elements, who may gain power and who in any case naturally sympathise with the Soviet Union and form a fifth column within individual States, prepared, as the Canadian spy case has shown, to put the interests of the Soviet Union above those of its own country. The Soviet Union cannot resist making use of such persons, fishing in troubled waters, and even appealing to them over the heads of the governments of States with whom it is in friendly relations and with whom it may even have alliances.

8. The above view of the outside world is sedulously propagated, despite much objective evidence that the picture is false. Recent history has shown that the Western democracies, far from uniting against the Soviet Union, contributed all the aid in their power in the common struggle against fascism. Far from wishing to encircle the Soviet Union, Britain and America have made, and are still making, every effort to increase intercourse between their countries and peoples and those of the Soviet Union, and to bring the Soviet Union fully into the world community. They have made concession after concession to encourage such cooperation, but so far with little response.

9. This brings us to the very important questions: Who are the real rulers of Russia propagating the above views, and how do their processes of thought really run in regard to the outside world? Ultimate power resides in the small circle of the Politburo, who have complete control of the military machine and of the ubiquitous and immensely powerful system of State security. The

natural assumption is that Stalin is, in fact, a dictator as absolute as Hitler in Germany. There is little doubt that the last word rests with him; but we have so often found that views expressed by him in private conversation are belied by subsequent events, that it would seem either that he is exceptionally crafty in dealing with foreign statesmen or that he is himself dependent upon the collective decisions of his colleagues in the Politburo. The explanation may even lie deeper, in the information or lack of information which reaches him about the outside world. Many foreign observers in Moscow consider that, although Molotov is publicly recognised as the second personality in the Soviet State, in fact greater power is wielded behind the scenes by Malenkov, who largely controls the Communist party machine, and by Beriya, until recently the head of the State security system and now promoted to a general supervision of the machinery of government. Some well-informed students of the Soviet Union have speculated that there may be a growing circle of ambitious Red Army men and industrial executives who, knowing nothing of the outside world, are ready to risk a trial of strength with their former allies in pursuing an adventurous foreign policy. But this is mere speculation, and it would be safer to assume that control is firmly in the hands of Stalin, as advised by his fellow members of the Politburo and more particularly by Molotov, Malenkov and Beriya.

10. It is hard to say whether these men share the view of the outside world sedulously propagated in Communist party propaganda. But it would, I think, be safer to assume that, brought up in the pure Marxist doctrine from earliest manhood and for the most part ignorant of the outside world, and having no real contacts even with leaders of other nations, they do, in fact, believe their own dogma. All their training—first as underground revolutionaries and then as the rulers of a State working against the greatest internal difficulties and facing the hostility of the world—must make them suspicious and, insofar as they are themselves with no friendly feelings towards the Western democracies and with no scruples whatsoever in dealing with them, they no doubt attribute similar motives to their opposite numbers in London and Washington, more particularly when they see in London representatives of social democracy and of the Second

International, with whom they have fought a long and bitter struggle, inside and outside the Soviet Union.

11. In determining Soviet policy Stalin and his colleagues have certain advantages over their opposite numbers elsewhere. They are less burdened with day-to-day problems. They do not have to justify themselves before Parliament and public opinion. And they have an opportunity of planning a long-term policy which is often denied to democratic parliamentary governments. It would now appear that Stalin, in fact, passed his vacation at Sachi last autumn in planning the Soviet foreign and democratic policy which is causing us anxiety today. In his projects for building up the military and economic strength of the Soviet Union, as announced in his February election speech and developed in the first of three new Five-Year Plans put before the Supreme Soviet on the 15th of March, he is planning ahead in terms of ten, fifteen and even twenty years in a way which would be difficult in another country.

12. But the Soviet rulers would seem to have one great disadvantage in dealing with the outside world. They seem to [be] genuinely ill- or mis-informed about what goes on elsewhere. Their sources of information are (a) an ill-experienced, frightened and overworked diplomatic service, whose members probably do not dare to say anything which might cause offence to the Kremlin even if they are themselves able to form an objective view of the countries in which they are posted; and (b) a fifth column of Communists, fellow travellers and misguided idealists, who must convey to their Soviet friends a very strange and often excessively rose-coloured picture of the position in their respective countries. Although it may seem odd, it is indeed probable that such persons as Mr. Harry Pollitt, the Dean of Canterbury and Mr. Priestley are relied upon in Moscow for an objective picture of political developments in Britain. And even this defective information is filtered carefully through to Stalin by innumerable party and government authorities culminating in Malenkov, Beriya and Molotov, all of whom, no doubt, twist and censor it to suit their own interests and preconceived ideas. When finally we consider that all Communists, from the top to the bottom, have a conception of the outside world based upon what they have learnt in the works of Marx, Lenin and Stalin, and subconsciously fit all developments into this ideological pattern, it will be realised that

the chances of the Soviet rulers being well informed upon the world situation are extremely slender, more particularly in view of their limited contacts with their opposite numbers in other countries. It is, indeed, possible that in any given crisis in international relations—as for example the recent Canadian spy case—a small group of high Communists or NKVD [People's Commissariat of Internal Affairs] officials might cover up their own clumsiness by convincing Stalin that what appeared like Soviet espionage was, in fact, only a further example of the determination of the outside capitalist world to stage a major anti-Soviet demonstration.

13. But however well- or ill-informed the Kremlin may be on the situation in the outside world it is certainly incapable, in conducting international relations, of the give-and-take which is normal and, indeed, essential between other States. When British delegates negotiate an agreement with delegates from any country other than the Soviet Union, there is usually an honest endeavour on both sides to understand the point of view of the other and to arrive at an agreement which must to some extent represent a compromise between the interests of both. Once this compromise has been achieved there is a certain finality about the agreement reached which is intended to cover relations between the two countries on this particular issue for some time to come, at least until the time when new negotiations are required. This, in its turn, implies a reasonable fidelity to the spirit as well as to the letter of international contracts and treaty obligations. Without this minimum of goodwill and good faith international relations, even on their present relatively low plane of morality, would be impossible in our sense of the term. The Soviet Union, however, does not conceive international relations in this sense at all. She approaches a partner, whom she regards as potentially hostile, endeavours to exact the maximum advantage for the Soviet Union, if possible without any return, and, having obtained what she wants, reopens this issue or raises another at the earliest possible moment in order to achieve the next item on her programme. There is, therefore, no degree of finality about any agreement reached with the Soviet Union, despite her much vaunted fidelity to her international obligations—the true value of which has recently been shown in Persia. All nations are, of course, guided by self-interest, but most other great nations

approach problems of common interest (e.g., the restoration of international trade, the provision of food for starving countries in Europe and the Far East) with a greater or a lesser desire to make their contribution and not only to exact the maximum advantage for themselves. There is among the other nations of the world a certain sense of world community, which is certainly not shown by the Soviet Union despite her new position in world affairs, which she has not only won for herself but been willingly accorded by her allies. Instead of encouraging increased contact between nations and dealing with them primarily as potential partners and not as ultimate enemies, the Soviet Union has since the war increased, if that were possible, the isolation of her people from outside influence, and her appearances on the international scene are publicly admitted here to be designed mainly to further the Soviet interests. In short, the Soviet Union is ideologically and economically a closed community, controlled by a small handful of men, themselves cut off from the outside world, whose system of government is based upon an all-pervasive police system and the most widespread propaganda machinery. Lest this may appear little more than an ideal generalisation, I attach annexes dealing very summarily with Soviet behaviour on certain specific problems affecting her relations with the outside world. [See appendixes I-IV at the end of section 2.]

14. In the light of these facts and of our recent experiences, one is driven to conclude not only that the rulers of the Soviet Union do not believe in the same things which Western democracies believe in, but that they are incapable of doing so. Reared as they have been in revolutionary traditions and impregnated with Marxist doctrine, they genuinely despise liberal ideas, tolerance, and the conceptions of right and justice which are the basis of Western thinking, however inadequately they may be interpreted in practice. The small group ruling Russia believe that the end justifies the means, and that they are at the head of a chosen people, or rather a chosen group of peoples, with a chosen system destined to spread throughout the world. In their view relations with the outside world and even alliances are short-term arrangements for definite objectives, and can be modified or rejected as soon as they no longer suit the purpose of the Soviet Union. From Marxist-Leninist doctrine springs absolute confidence in the future of the Soviet State and system, deep suspicion

and distrust of the outside world and complete disregard for all personal considerations and normal human relationships between individuals and States alike.

15. It is no use disguising the fact that the above situation is alarming. But there are, fortunately, other factors to be taken into account. Apart from a certain feeling of xenophobia based upon the conviction that they have not hitherto had their fair share of the good things of the world, the peoples of the Soviet Union, and above all the dominant Russian people, are not naturally hostile to the outside world, nor eager to dominate other peoples. The intelligentsia are friendly, cultivated and clever, and only too anxious to meet similar persons from other countries and to measure their wits against them. The masses are, for the most part, friendly, capable of sudden bursts of fury in which no excuse can be found for their behaviour but, as all foreigners in the Soviet Union can testify, fundamentally eager for good relations with the outside world and ready to be influenced by foreign ideas and foreign contacts. This is therefore a people very different from the Germans, who regarded themselves as a master race, destined to dominate the world, and who fully sympathised with the ruthless and ambitious policies of their leaders. In addition, there is a fundamental streak of laziness, indiscipline and inefficiency running through the Russian people, who must be constantly kept up to the mark if they are to preserve their position in the world. Granted these national characteristics, it is essential that the Soviet people should be ruled with the greatest firmness and, at the same time, deceived about the outside world. A foreign bogey and the fear of foreign aggression must be held before them to stimulate their efforts for the new Five-Year Plan, and to persuade them that a large proportion of these efforts must be devoted, not to improving the lot of the Soviet people, but to preparing either for the defence of the Soviet Union or for future expansion.

16. Another important, although somewhat speculative, consideration is how far the Revolution has stabilised itself in the Soviet Union. There is no doubt that the present Soviet regime is fully accepted by the overwhelming majority of the Soviet peoples. Large sections of the population now have a stake in the regime and all those under 40 know of nothing else. In fact, Soviet Russia has reached a similar stage in development as revolutionary France when the First Empire had become solidly established.

Although Soviet Russia intends to spread her influence by all possible means, world revolution is no longer part of her programme and there is nothing in internal conditions within the Union which might encourage a return to the old revolutionary traditions.

17. Any comparison between the German menace before the war and a Soviet menace today must also allow for the following fundamental differences:

(a) In the first place, the Soviet Union, unlike Germany, is a vast territory containing all the primary products necessary for a modern State and with more than enough scope for all the energies of its peoples in developing these vast resources. There is plenty of room for a population far larger than the present 190 million, and the greater part of the Soviet Union is backward and undeveloped. Although, therefore, Soviet energies are as dynamic as those of Germany, there is not the same motive force compelling the Soviet Union to burst out beyond its frontiers and carve out for itself its due place in the world.

(b) Moreover, the rulers of Russia are infinitely more flexible than those of Germany. However much they may be wedded to Marxist doctrine, this allows them considerable latitude in regard to tactics and timing. Whereas the Germans set themselves a definite goal to be achieved within a given time regardless of opposition and changes in the international situation, the Russians are capable of readjusting their projects if faced by opposition or unexpected difficulties. They do not charge into brick walls, even when they have the necessary strength to break them down, but prefer to wait and find some means of either getting round or climbing over the wall. There is, therefore, infinitely less danger of sudden catastrophe with the Russians than with the Germans.

(c) Furthermore, the rulers of Russia have not got the same sense of urgency as Hitler, who knew that if Germany was to dominate Europe and the world she must act quickly. The Kremlin, on the other hand, is confident that time is on its side and there is, therefore, no need to prejudice certain future progress by pressing ahead too sharply or rapidly with any particular project.

(d) Soviet Russia is also largely free from any sense of racial superiority or of a mission to dominate the world, though there is a certain Messianic strain in the Russian outlook. Her methods are much more subtle and they aim at the ultimate creation of a communist or socialist society throughout the world in close communion of spirit with the Soviet Union. They do not call for open conquest and least of all for the launching of a war of aggression, except possibly for limited aims.

(e) Finally, the internal position inside the Soviet Union, and in particular the economic structure, is at present much weaker than might be imagined if one listened only to Soviet propaganda. The internal problems facing the Soviet Union are quite as serious as those facing the Western democracies and they are on an even larger scale, while there is infinitely more leeway to make up in assuring even a modest standard of life to the now expectant Soviet people. The advent of the atomic bomb has shown that the Soviet military machine is by no means invincible, and the rulers of Russia know very well the inadequacy of the Red navy and air forces. They also know that there are strong forces throughout the world—American capitalism, British social democracy and the Catholic Church among them—which would form strong centres of opposition to any attempt by the Soviet Union in the immediate future to dominate the world. In fact, the Soviet Union, although confident in its ultimate strength, is nothing like so strong at present as the Western democratic world, and knows it.

18. On the morrow of the greatest Russian victories in history, the rulers of the Soviet Union have seen their opportunity to achieve their ambitions, unless they are thwarted by the capitalist world uniting against them again and trumping what seemed the Red Army ace with the even better card of the atomic bomb. Basically, the Kremlin is now pursuing a Russian national policy which does not differ except in degree from that pursued in the past by Ivan the Terrible, Peter the Great or Catherine the Great. But what would, in other lands, be naked imperialism or power politics is covered by the more attractive garb of Marxist-Leninist ideology, which, in its turn, moulds the approach to world problems of statesmen whose belief in their own ideology is as profound as that of the Jesuits in their own faith during the Counter Reformation. This long-term policy would appear to fall under six main heads:

(a) In the first place every effort is being made to develop the Soviet Union into the most powerful State in the world, if necessary by its own unaided efforts, and meanwhile to provide for

Soviet security. This means that at a time when other countries are busy demobilising and reducing their armed forces, the Soviet Union is maintaining a very large military establishment, modernising its equipment and industrial base, and hesitating even to reduce its garrison forces abroad, which probably number at least three million men. The search for security is a constantly expanding process. The establishment of the Soviet frontier on the Curzon Line has meant that a puppet Polish State must have its frontiers on the Oder and the Neisse. This, in its turn, leads to Soviet control of the eastern zone of Germany through a faithful Communist party, and to encouragement of Communist influence in the rest of Germany and even in France. To take another example, the domination of Persian Azerbaijan to protect the oil in Baku leads on naturally to the domination of Persia as a whole, to encouragement of a puppet Kurdish republic, to the isolation of Turkey and eventually to infiltration into the whole Arab world. A legitimate demand for a large say in the control of the Dardanelles is at once followed by demands for bases in the Dodecanese and Tripolitania. In fact, Soviet security has become hard to distinguish from Soviet imperialism and it is becoming uncertain whether there is, in fact, any limit to Soviet expansion.

(b) The second and connected objective is to weaken capitalist or social-democratic countries in every way. So far as Britain is concerned, this means the encouragement of "national liberation movements" in India, throughout the colonial world, and in the Middle East. It also means constant intrigue against and undermining of our established position in Scandinavia, Western Europe, the Iberian Peninsula and Greece. Any tendency on the part of Western European countries to draw closer together will be bitterly opposed. In Britain itself the Communist party and fellow travellers will be used as a spearhead to undermine the mistrusted forces of social democracy now dominant with the Labour Government. Any discomfiture we may suffer anywhere in the world will be seized upon and exploited.

(c) Everything possible will be done to keep the Americans and ourselves apart.

(d) Although the Communist International no longer exists, Communist parties everywhere will be supported and used to further Soviet interests, and ultimately to take over the government. Nongovernmental international organisations such as the

World Federation of Trade Unions and international youth and women's organisations will also be encouraged and used for Soviet political ends.

(e) Social democracy and all moderate progressive forces will everywhere be attacked bitterly and ruthlessly as the main dangers to communism and so to the Soviet Union. These forces are regarded not so much as an ultimate alternative to communism but rather as an opiate for the workers, who, after they have received certain limited benefits which social democracy can offer, will no longer have the necessary incentive to carry through the revolution within their own countries. In this sense, therefore, social democracy will always be regarded as a tool for capitalism and reaction.

(f) Finally, and perhaps most important at the moment, the full weight of Soviet propaganda, and where possible active support, will be brought to bear in favour of the so-called oppressed colonial peoples and against imperialist domination. This is in line with orthodox Marxist teaching, as well as with Soviet national interests, and there is little doubt that the Soviet peoples, from Stalin downwards, are embarking upon such a campaign with the zeal of crusaders and with a sincere belief that they are thereby contributing to the progress of the world.

19. In the heat of the current controversies and so soon after the end of the war it is difficult to determine with certainty how far these policies represent mainly a tactical short-term campaign designed (a) to get the maximum advantages for the Soviet Union in the present fluid state of international society, and (b) to intimidate us into renewed cooperation with the Soviet Union, but on their own terms, and how far it is a long-term strategy. With a regime whose ultimate ambitions, although not its immediate aims, are unlimited and which views the world as a whole *sub specie aeternitatis*, much as the Catholic Church might do, policy is probably not so clear-cut and the contrast between short-term tactics and long-term strategy may be unreal. At all events we should be wise to frame our own policy on the assumptions

(i) That the Soviet regime is dynamic and that the Soviet Union is still expanding, although admittedly not as yet beyond areas where Russian interests existed before the Revolution;

(ii) That her long-term ambitions are dangerous to vital British interests as we now see them;

(iii) That security is the first consideration with the Soviet Union and that she will not endanger the realisation of her long-term projects by pressing immediate issues to the point of serious conflict, except as the result of a miscalculation of forces;

(iv) That it is therefore possible, though difficult, to reconcile British and Soviet interests in any problem with which we are likely to be faced, granted the right mixture of strength and patience and the avoidance of sabre-rattling or the raising of prestige issues; but

(v) That, except in the now unlikely event of Germany or some other Power again becoming a deadly menace to British and Russian survival, there is no longer in the new international situation any certainty of Britain and Russia being automatically drawn together in major international crises, as we were in 1812, 1914 and 1941.

I am sending a copy of this despatch to His Majesty's Ambassador at Washington.

I have, &c.
F.K. ROBERTS

Appendix I

Attitude to the United Nations Organisation

It must at once be admitted that the Soviet Government, whose basic attitude to the United Nations Organisation is mentioned in paragraph 4 of the covering despatch, have worked hard and made valuable contributions to the establishment of the United Nations Organisation. But from the very beginning, and more particularly in regard to the veto, they have insisted that the United Nations Organisation could never be used against Soviet interests. They have constantly pressed for representation in the United Nations Organisation for outside bodies in which Soviet influence is very strong, e.g., the World Federation of Trade Unions and the international youth and women's movements. These claims, if granted, would make it easier for the Soviet Union to appeal to other peoples over the heads of their governments and authorised representatives at the United Nations Organisation. Already at the San Francisco Conference last April Molotov, when pledging Soviet support for the new organisation, gave a clear warning that while the Soviet Union wanted it to succeed, she had other strings to her bow and was quite prepared to turn to other methods for retaining and spreading Soviet influence in the world if the United Nations Organisation did not come up to Soviet expectations. The recent London meeting of the General Assembly and Security Council provided an excellent example of the Soviet attitude to the United Nations Organisation. It is evidently to be used as a forum in which Soviet representatives can cover up high-handed Soviet actions and embarrass other countries by irresponsible charges designed to curry favour with the so-called oppressed peoples. Even in procedural and non-political questions the Soviet representatives were constantly finding themselves supporting (to us) untenable theses and were heavily out-voted. In fact, the Soviet conception of international negotiations, whether in the United Nations Organisation, the Council of Foreign Ministers or between the Big Three, consists not so much of arriving at agreement as in reaching agreement exclusively on Soviet terms. Insofar as the Soviet people and possibly even the small circle of the rulers sincerely believe that they are the sole repositories of justice and right-thinking in the world, their representatives have no doubt returned from London with a sense of grievance and isolation which is not encouraging for the future of world cooperation.

Appendix II

Intellectual Exchanges and Personal Contacts

Never since the Revolution has the Soviet Union been so cut off from the outside world as today. Apart from a handful of American engineers installing oil refineries, and for a larger number of Communists and fellow travellers whose natural centre is Moscow, the only foreigners in the Soviet Union today are the diplomatic corps in Moscow, a dwindling body of foreign correspondents, and Axis prisoners of war who have not yet been released. The diplomatic corps and the correspondents are more carefully shepherded and more strictly segregated from all normal contacts with Russians than at any previous period, despite Stalin's repeated statements to British representatives that he does not desire such segregation. Constant endeavours by His Majesty's Government in London and through this embassy to encourage an exchange of visits between the two countries, to exchange teachers and students in order to promote real knowledge of each country by the other, have all been fruitless, if not actively discouraged. Cultural contacts are canalised through VOKS [Soviet Union Society for Cultural Relations with Foreign Countries], an institution whose purpose is to restrict rather than to encourage exchanges of knowledge and the promotion of real friendship. Meanwhile, specially selected visitors, usually fellow travellers like the Dean of Canterbury or Mr. Priestley, are brought to this country, lavishly entertained and sent back to do Soviet propaganda in Britain. When by rare chance representative, honest and friendly visitors, such as the British Iron and Steel delegation, reach the Soviet Union and afterwards make some frank but friendly criticisms imbued with a genuine admiration for many aspects of Soviet life, they are branded as tools of reactionaries, if not as plain fascist beasts. Conversely, the only Russians allowed out of the Soviet Union are persons carefully vetted by the regime who can be relied upon not to form an objective impression of the countries they visit, but to do Soviet propaganda there and to return to Russia with enough adverse material to inspire unfavorable press comment in Moscow. Although private individuals and government spokesmen alike in Britain and the United States plead for the doors to be opened, these appeals pass unheeded on the Soviet side, and I know of no single step which they have taken parallel to the innumerable efforts from our side to encourage free, frank and friendly intercourse between Soviet citizens and their counterparts in the Western democracies. The experiences of our prisoners of war repatriated through the Soviet Union and of our troops wherever they have met the Red Army face to face in Europe have more than borne out the experience of foreign residents in Moscow.

Appendix III

Trade Policy

The Soviet attitude to international trade is to obtain certain essential products, if possible on credit, but to rely mainly upon her own resources for the reconstruction and development of the Soviet Union. She has no general interest in increasing commercial exchanges between nations. She certainly does not regard international trade as a means of bringing the nations together and of increasing prosperity throughout the world. What she intends to do is to build up the economic strength of the Soviet Union and to indulge only in the limited degree of foreign trade necessary for that purpose. Her attitude to Bretton Woods and to the American proposals for an international trade and tariff conference has therefore been purely negative. Although she would like an American and even a British loan, or credit, she has not so far shown herself ready to lift a finger to encourage either the Americans or ourselves to make such a loan or credit and is certainly not ready to accept any awkward conditions for it. Throughout the whole of Eastern Europe the Soviet Union is carrying out a sort of Schacht plan in reverse, under which the countries within the Soviet orbit will find their economies increasingly geared to Soviet needs and to the Soviet Five-Year Plan. Foreign interests meanwhile are being frozen out and discouraged in every way from playing a part in the economic life of Eastern Europe, except, of course, when it comes to giving charity through UNRRA [United Nations Relief and Rehabilitation Administration] with no countervailing advantages to the benefactor countries. On the other hand, the Soviet Union has no designs at present to compete on any scale in the world export markets and, once normal conditions return, a limited and mutually profitable Anglo-Soviet trade in goods essential to both parties can no doubt be resumed.

Appendix IV

Press Censorship and Presentation of News

In no country, not even in Nazi Germany, has there been such a dishonest presentation of world news and such a dangerous censorship of foreign correspondents as there is today in the Soviet Union. World news reproduced in the Soviet press is carefully selected to fit into whatever happens to be the propaganda pattern of the day. The most important declarations of policy and developments are, if necessary, completely ignored or, alternatively, presented to the Soviet public in such a twisted form as to give an entirely misleading impression. On the other hand, minor items of no possible importance or interest are played up. I need not quote instances of this, as the Foreign Office files are already full of them. Meanwhile, the press censorship in Moscow works in such a way that only items favourable to the Soviet Union can be telegraphed out of the country; while more recently the Soviet censorship has taken to deciding itself not merely what is not to be said, but what is to be said, without even informing correspondents of what is going out over their signatures. The Soviet public is therefore constantly and systematically misled about the world situation, persuaded either that friends are enemies or that criticism is really applause. Similarly, the general public outside the Soviet Union receives an incomplete and misleading picture of developments here. At any given moment Soviet action and policy can be presented in the most favourable light, while those of the Western democracies are traduced and misrepresented.

Moscow, March 18, 1946, Section 3

It remains to consider the most important question of all: what British policy should be towards the Soviet Union if the assessment of Soviet policy attempted in my despatch No. 189 is approximately correct.

2. We have tried many methods in the recent past. After a brief attempt at the beginning of the Revolution to work with the new regime in order to keep Russia in the war, we tried armed intervention and the support of separatist movements throughout the Russian Empire in order to break down the Soviet regime and ensure its replacement by some government more akin to other European governments. This failed lamentably, and not even the most stubborn and shortsighted reactionaries would advocate another attempt at foreign intervention today. There then followed a period of isolation, during which there were no diplomatic relations between the Soviet Union and the greater part of the outside world. From the other side of a *cordon sanitaire* we watched with little sympathy the painful efforts of the Soviet Government to restore some sort of order and a passable standard of living within the shattered Russian Empire. On her side, the Soviet Union still propagated world revolution through the Comintern. As it became clear that the Soviet regime had come to stay, diplomatic relations were opened, but it was not until the thirties, when the common German danger brought the Soviet Union into the League of Nations in the pursuit of collective security, that anything approaching normality existed between London and Moscow. The failure of the attempt to achieve collective security, the bitter memories of the Spanish civil war and of Munich (regarded by the Soviet Union as a betrayal by the West), and finally the Soviet counter-betrayal in the Soviet-German pact of 1939 brought to nothing what had seemed a promising experiment. Then came the German attack upon the Soviet Union, the Anglo-Soviet Alliance of 1942, the growth of Big Three cooperation, and finally the victory over Germany and Japan and the creation of the United Nations Organisation. During this last period Anglo-Soviet cooperation and relative confidence was built up slowly and painfully, with many setbacks, and by last summer a solid foundation appeared to have been achieved and

there seemed reason to hope that the Soviet Union might settle down into a more or less normal member of international society, and that Anglo-Soviet relations could become progressively more intimate and more trusting. But unfortunately this last period was in no sense typical. Apart from the fact that we were both fighting for our lives and were therefore compelled to cooperate, all the concessions, approaches and even gestures came from our side, and the Kremlin must have found the course of Anglo-Soviet relations a very pleasant and convenient arrangement under which they received big gains, though it must be remembered that in Russian eyes at least the Soviet Union had borne the main burden of the war. They probably hoped and expected that this would continue after the war, and the present crisis in our relations is largely due to a realisation on both sides that the time for one-sided appeasement and concession is past.

3. It is easier to draw the conclusion that none of the methods adopted over the past thirty years should be repeated than to put forward any very positive or inspiring substitute for them. I would, however, suggest that the first essential is to treat the problem of Anglo-Soviet relations in the same way as major military problems were treated during the war. It calls for the closest coordination of political strategy, for a very thorough staff study embracing every aspect of Soviet policy—not forgetting the ubiquitous activities of the Communist parties directed, if not controlled in detail, from Moscow.

4. Of no other country is it harder to know the true position or to form an unbiased judgement. Hence the necessity not only for full factual information but for a readiness to face the facts and all their implications, however unpleasant they may appear at first sight.

5. Parallel with this should go a campaign to educate the British public with whom all decisions of policy ultimately rest. In the case of other important countries, the British public, or at least influential sections of it, have real knowledge on which to base their judgments. In the case of the Soviet Union alone they are dependent upon either Soviet propaganda or anti-Soviet prejudices, which are equally dangerous counsellors. Insofar as normal contacts do not exist between the Soviet and British publics and are unlikely to be permitted by the Soviet Government, and as even press correspondents in Moscow can only send

out news censored by the Soviet authorities (and already coloured by their own fears lest frankness might forfeit them a subsequent visa for the Soviet Union), the responsibility for educating the British public must rest with His Majesty's Government and the editors in London to an extent which would be altogether abnormal in dealing with other countries.

6. The most essential factor in our long-term strategy is, however, to ensure that our own country, the Commonwealth, the Colonial Empire and those countries—particularly in Western Europe and the Near and Middle East—whose fortunes are so closely bound up with ours should be healthy political and economic organisms, pursuing progressive policies, raising the standard of living of their peoples, and removing the causes of social strife. At the same time we can offer civil and personal liberties which are unknown in the Soviet Union and would be the envy of its inhabitants. In fact, we should act as the champions of a dynamic and progressive faith and way of life with an appeal to the world at least as great as that of the Communist system of the Kremlin. The Soviet Union would not, I fear, in the long run resist the temptation to infiltrate into and encroach upon a weak British Empire which was on the defensive and a prey to internal troubles and dissensions. Moreover, the Communist system propagated from Moscow thrives best in unhealthy organisms. But as long as we can offer our peoples and the world at large economic, social and political benefits which are still far from being realised in the Soviet Union itself, we can reasonably hope for the maintenance of Anglo-Soviet relations on a basis of mutual respect and regard for each other's interests.

7. Turning from strategy to tactics, it is essential to realise that there is no shortcut to good Anglo-Soviet relations. From time to time personal contacts may be necessary—either in the United Nations Organisation, between the Big Five or the Big Three, or between Britain and the Soviet Union alone. But although these personal contacts may solve some immediate problem, they can never be relied upon to influence Soviet policy in the future, least of all to provide a solid basis for relations. The day has also long gone when we might hope by unilateral gestures or concessions on our side gradually to influence Soviet policy and so to inspire similar gestures and concessions from the Soviet side. In dealing with the Soviet Union, as indeed with the old Russian Empire, we

should base ourselves firmly on the principle of reciprocity and give nothing unless we receive a counter-advantage in return. This in turn implies great firmness in dealing with big matters and small alike, coupled, however, with a friendly approach, with perfect politeness and with a formal correctness, which we may no longer consider necessary in our dealings with other countries in this democratic age. In these respects the old should be mixed with the new diplomacy in the conduct of our relations with the Soviet Union, both in regard to secrecy and also to outward forms. When there are deadlocks, as there will often be, we should cultivate the same patience as is shown by our Soviet allies, and cease to feel that it is always our task to make an early gesture to break the deadlock. Such gestures are interpreted here as a sign of weakness and do harm rather than good to our relations. However unpromising the prospects may be, we should, however, continue to take the initiative in fostering closer contacts between the two peoples, e.g., cultural and other exchanges and visits by representative persons and delegations. Visitors to the Soviet Union should, however, be carefully chosen and this implies a certain degree of control, such as is exercised by the Soviet Union over visitors to Britain, in order to ensure that it is not only Communists and fellow travellers selected by the Russians who bring as false an impression of Britain to the Soviet people as the picture of the Soviet Union which they take back with them. As a part of this campaign of mutual education, we should continue to support our one regular means of propaganda in the Soviet Union—the *British Ally*—and foster with the greatest care the BBC programmes in Russian which are about to begin. Finally, we should in our mutual interest restore at the earliest possible moment normal trade between the two countries. But this should be done on a basis of mutual needs and not of one-sided loans or other concessions, and we should clearly realise that Anglo-Soviet trade is unlikely to become a major factor in our relations, or in the international commercial balance as a whole.

8. In all our dealings with the Soviet Union we should constantly bear in mind the absolute need for earning and maintaining respect. This means that we must be strong and look strong. But this strength should never be paraded unnecessarily and it should always take account of Soviet susceptibilities and prestige. Above all, we should never rattle the sabre and make it difficult

for the Russians to climb down without loss of face. It is significant that Soviet propaganda has reacted very sharply to Mr. Churchill's frank statement at Fulton on the Soviet respect for strength. But, as some highly placed Russians told a diplomatic colleague, they do not object to the ideas expressed by Mr. Churchill, even when he advocated the closest relations between Britain and America. They felt, however, that it was unnecessary and undesirable to state these obvious facts in public in a way which appeared to many Russians as provocative.

9. If we are to be strong, this, of course, implies cherishing our special relationship with the Dominions and also with America, fostering the natural community of interests between ourselves and the democracies of Western Europe, and supporting and strengthening our friends and allies in the Middle East. I cannot lay too much emphasis upon maintaining our special relationship with America in a form consistent with friendship with the Soviet Union. Whatever private differences may arise between us, America and the British Commonwealth must remain firm friends in the eyes of the Soviet Union, otherwise she may succumb to dangerous temptations. The Soviet Union cannot legitimately object to such developments, which have no aggressive tendencies against her, although she will no doubt use her influence to retard them. Indeed, if we were thinking simply in terms of Anglo-Soviet relations, these could probably be most solidly established on the basis of zones of influence in which we each left the other party free from interference or criticism within specified areas.

10. I have not touched upon the problem of the United Nations Organisation in this context since I assume that we shall in any case continue to do all in our power to strengthen it, and this is, in any case, a problem much wider than that of Anglo-Soviet relations. If, however, we wish the United Nations Organisation to succeed, we must allow for the Soviet view that it can only do so on a basis of prior agreement on all important issues between the Big Three. Soviet behaviour may make this unattainable, in which event it might be wiser to accept the position and no longer to place what might prove a dangerous faith in the United Nations Organisation as a substitute for Big Three cooperation and for a reconciliation of British and Soviet interests.

11. I realise that the above may not seem a very inspiring policy and will indeed be a sad disappointment to those who had set their hopes of postwar Anglo-Soviet relations very high. But British relations with Russia were for three centuries maintained not unsuccessfully on such a basis of distant realism between governments. If we do not aim too high, we shall at least avoid constant irritations and disappointments. The many important interests we have in common, and most of all our joint determination that no other one Power shall ever become a menace to us both, should remain a solid bond, despite the deep gulf between our social systems.

I am sending a copy of this despatch to His Majesty's Ambassador at Washington.

I have, &c.

F.K. ROBERTS

Notes

1. At the top of the original of the document is the handwritten phrase "From N. Novikov" and a handwritten note, by Molotov, that he wished the document to be saved, presumably in his files or otherwise nearby, until January 1, 1947. The following citation accompanied the Russian manuscript of the document: AVP SSSR, f. 06, op. 8, p. 45, d. 759.

2. In the margin, Molotov has written in response to this sentence: "Otlichie ot dovoennogo?" that is, "A difference from [the] prewar [period]?"

3. This sentence gets a vertical line in the margin from Molotov and the word "cooperation" is underlined a second time.

4. This sentence gets two vertical lines in the margin from Molotov and "division of the world" is circled several times.

5. This sentence and the one before it receive two vertical lines in the margin from Molotov, plus an exclamation point, again in the margin.

6. The phrase "the division of the world in the Far East" is circled.

7. "Relations between the United States and England" is circled, and the first two sentences of this paragraph are marked across with a large check.

8. This sentence and the next are marked across with checks.

9. This sentence is marked across with a large check.

10. The underlined phrase is also marked across with a check.

11. In this telegram the State Department informed the chargé: "We should welcome receiving from you an interpretive analysis of what we may expect in the way of future implementation of these announced policies..." (861.00/2-1246). The policies referred to were those contained in the pre-election speeches of Stalin and his associates.

12. The Third (Communist) International, founded by the Bolsheviks at Moscow in March 1919, announced as having been dissolved in May 1943; see *Foreign Relations*, 1943, vol. III, pp. 531-32 and 542-43.

The Commentaries

Commentary

Viktor L. Mal'kov

The history of George Kennan's "Long Telegram" and of Nikolai Novikov's dispatch are not identical. Kennan's telegram was originally intended "only for the information of the president and the secretary of state" when it was sent on 22 February 1946. With the support and approval of the State Department, an extended version of the telegram was subsequently published in the journal *Foreign Affairs* as an anonymous article entitled "The Sources of Soviet Conduct." Historians of American foreign relations agree that few documents have had as much influence in official circles as did the "Long Telegram." Not surprisingly, it has given birth to a whole body of research throughout the world, and to this day the telegram is seen as a key document in the conceptual formation of the American policy of containment.

Alongside Kennan's telegram there is now another document—the Novikov dispatch—that analyzes "the foreign policy of the United States in the postwar period." Novikov, the Soviet ambassador to the United States, prepared this document at the request of Soviet foreign minister V. M. Molotov on 27 September 1946. The dispatch was made public only in 1990 at a conference of Soviet and American specialists on the "Conduct of the Cold War." This conference took place both in Moscow and in Washington from May to July 1990 and was jointly organized by the center for organization and scientific coordination of the Soviet Ministry of Foreign Affairs and the U.S.-based Institute of Peace. The declassification of the Novikov dispatch was finally made possible by changes in the archival policy of the Soviet Union during 1990. Both the Kennan and Novikov documents are highly significant for what they reveal about the foreign policies of the United States and the Soviet Union and about how each of these countries perceived the other at the onset of the Cold War.

It is clear that Kennan's telegram received high praise and approval precisely because those officials who read it already shared in and agreed with its ideological framework and interpretations. By the time the "Long Telegram" arrived in Washington, American leaders had embarked on a new approach to foreign policy. They had abandoned the wartime coalition, with its stress on cooperation with Great Britain and the Soviet Union, in favor of a policy based on a bipolar view of the world and confrontation with the Soviet Union. Kennan's telegram thus served less to reorient U.S. policy than to provide a clear, articulate justification for an analytical framework in which to place a reorientation that had occurred earlier. In exactly the same way, Novikov's dispatch was preceded by a series of statements by representatives of the Soviet leadership that also signaled a shift toward a bipolar world view with an emphasis on confrontation with the United States. Both Molotov's famous speech of 6 February 1946 and his statements about the outcome of the Paris conference of foreign ministers, which were published in the Moscow newspapers on 27 May 1946, reflect this new confrontational foreign policy.

Thus, in the Soviet Union and in the United States, a particular worldview and analytical framework had been established prior to the writing of the Kennan and Novikov documents. This new analytical framework led to important generalizations on the part of officials in both countries and produced in both a similar, essentially confrontational foreign policy. Confrontation escalated as each side pursued a diplomacy that aimed to counter the perceived expansionism of the other. For Kennan, evidence of Soviet expansionism and the principal danger to American values was to be found in the worldwide subversive activities of Communist parties under Soviet influence. For Novikov, proof of American expansionism was evident in the reemergence of militarism in the United States and in the American drive to establish a global system of military bases. The foreign policy of each country was proclaimed by the other to be a quest for world hegemony. Although Novikov and, in particular, Kennan expressed qualifications, the general picture of the world they painted was essentially the same: a dichotomous cleavage—on one side the powers of good, on the other, evil.

It is important when studying historical documents to remember that even though a document appears after certain events it is not necessarily because of those events that it was written. It is indisputable that certain developments that preceded Novikov's dispatch, such as Winston Churchill's speech at Fulton, Missouri, on 6 March 1946, the periodic American flexing of its atomic muscles, and the escalating intensity of the debates in the United States about the probability of a third world war, all influenced the development of Novikov's views. But it is also important to recognize that ideology was rapidly becoming the dominant factor shaping Soviet thinking about foreign policy in the years following the end of the war. A preconceived ideological schema began to imprison the Soviet diplomatic service and to make it difficult for diplomats to respond accurately to the rapidly changing circumstances and the new events and historical trends that characterized the postwar era. This "blinkering" of thought guided even the hand of Molotov, and is shown by the series of underlinings he made in the text of Novikov's dispatch.

It is necessary to clarify the authorship of the dispatch. Molotov was, in reality, an anonymous co-author, a point Novikov stressed in his *Recollections of a Diplomat*, published in 1989.[1] The very idea of preparing an essay on the goals of American foreign policy originated with Molotov during the heated debates of the 1946 Paris peace conference. The impetus for Molotov's decision to prepare the essay was the fierce confrontation that characterized the conference, especially the verbal duel between the Soviet and American delegations, in which each side sought to overwhelm its opponent and to gain a propaganda advantage by mobilizing the world press. Molotov expressed the dissatisfaction of the Soviet delegation with the way the conference had been conducted, with its results, and with its low level of "authoritativeness," by which he meant the ability of the Western delegations to use their majority to overrule the wishes of the Soviet Union and thus to prevent the conference from truly representing the combined views of all of the participants.[2]

The mood of the conference was hostile from the beginning. Despite a few positive moments, negotiations proceeded with difficulty in an atmosphere of mutual reproach. The Soviet delegation, which included Novikov, rapidly developed a fortress mentality and felt besieged on all sides, a situation that Molotov thought needed special explanation. As a result, Molotov ordered Novikov to write an essay for the members of the delegation. The preliminary draft was to be given to Molotov first. Although it is not known what comments Molotov made about the essay, it is known from Novikov's memoirs that during the discussions of the rough draft Molotov clearly expressed his views regarding the content and thrust of the final document.

Having been rushed in the completion of the document, Novikov was himself dissatisfied with the result, as were several of his colleagues. They argued that the document emphasized the wrong points and that it therefore lacked the precision and clarity necessary to give a proper presentation of the abrupt shift of American foreign policy away from cooperation and toward preparation for war against the Soviet Union. In the autumn of 1947, when Novikov's dismissal as ambassador was being actively considered, the deficiencies of his analysis of postwar American foreign policy were cited as a major reason to relieve him. The criticisms of Novikov's interpretation were based on already existing perceptions as to the nature of the new bipolar world. Novikov's detractors sought to justify their ideology by updating their analysis to fit recent events. They emphasized that the historical dialectic was pushing the United States and the Soviet Union toward a military confrontation.

Thus, at the beginning of October 1947, a document appeared in Moscow that had also originated at the Soviet embassy in Washington.[3] The document contained an analysis of Novikov's earlier dispatch by an anonymous but highly placed diplomat who warned Molotov that Novikov's dispatch "[did] not reveal the real state of affairs in [the United States]."[4] The central problem was said to be Novikov's limited and superficial judgment, which prevented him from accurately assessing the driving forces and motives behind American policy toward the Soviet Union. Novikov's argument that U.S. foreign policy aimed at blackmail and intimidation of the Soviet Union was rejected. Instead, the document asserted that the goal of U.S. policy was the direct preparation for war against the Soviet Union.

Furthermore, if the United States appeared in the future to be abandoning its preparations for war and embarking on a quest for mutual accommodation with the Soviet Union, such a policy should be interpreted as merely a tactical maneuver, made necessary by the internal pressure of public opinion, and not as an indication of any real change in U.S. objectives. That preparation for war was the primary policy of the United States was clearly shown by the American "disinclination to move toward an agreement in the question of atomic energy" and by "the efforts to begin to resolve the German and Japanese questions to the detriment of the security of the Soviet Union and in the direction of the conversion of those countries into a staging ground for military aggression against the USSR."[5]

The author of the "alternative" analysis of U.S. foreign policy considered the question of war with the Soviet Union to have been "predetermined" by the powerful military party in the United States and by large American military appropriations in the immediate postwar period. With a few modifications, this interpretation of the American enemy, rather than Novikov's, was essentially repeated in all succeeding analyses sent to Moscow from the Soviet embassy in Washington.[6] Unlike Novikov's dispatch, all of these later documents stressed the threat of atomic war and the propaganda of military preparedness. But strictly speaking, all of these efforts, including Novikov's, were merely variations on the same theme. The bridges had already been burned, and each of the two superpowers, yesterday's allies, was now preparing for a long struggle to sustain a global order that seemed appropriate to its national interests and ideology.

In the Soviet Union, the United States was portrayed as an offensive, expansionist state, and the greatest problem for American expansionism was perceived to be the efforts of former colonial peoples to achieve genuine independence and national autonomy. The Truman Doctrine was interpreted within this framework, not surprisingly, because nobody in the world then considered Greece or Turkey to be examples of democracy. Truman's message to Congress coincided with the opening of the fourth session of the council of foreign ministers in Moscow (10 March–24 April 1947) and seemed to illustrate the thesis that Novikov and the rest of the Soviet embassy had been propounding. It seemed to prove that the strategic plans of the U.S. army and navy were offensive in character and that Secretary of State George C. Marshall was being disingenuous when he told Stalin on 15 April 1947 that he was "very much troubled and somewhat annoyed by the degree of mutual misunderstanding and disagreement that he detected in the course of the conference."[7] Marshall blamed these difficulties on the intractability of the Soviet delegation. Stalin rejected that allegation and claimed to be optimistic that relations would improve. He called the Moscow session a reconnaissance skirmish, and stated that compromise would become possible when both the United States and the Soviet Union had exhausted each other.[8]

For Novikov, who was present at this meeting, the Truman Doctrine and Marshall's comments were all part of yet another attempt by the United States to intimidate and pressure the Soviet Union into making concessions, an attempt that had again been thwarted. For all intents and purposes, compromise between the superpowers was no longer possible. Yet in Stalin's mind the rhetoric of compromise could still be useful in setting a good tone for U.S.-Soviet discussions, recalling as it did the memory of inter-Allied cooperation during the war. Truman, too, saw the political value of publicly speaking of possible compromise. Nevertheless, the very concept of compromise had been expunged from the framework of Soviet-American relations. The Cold War had begun, and the Kennan and Novikov documents were simply by-products of an already existing ideological framework based on confrontation. Their significance lies less in what changes in policy they brought about than in what they reveal about how the United States and the Soviet Union perceived each other at the beginning of the Cold War.

Notes

1. See Nikolai V. Novikov, *Vospominaniia diplomata: Zapiski 1938–1947* [Recollections of a diplomat: Memoirs 1938–1947] (Moscow, 1989), 353.

2. See V. M. Molotov, *Voprosy vneshnei politiki* [Questions of foreign policy] (Moscow, 1948), 227, 230, 231.

3. Archive of Foreign Affairs of the Soviet Union. Fond S-ta Ministra V. M. Molotova. Op. 9, i. 1041, p. 67.

4. Ibid.

5. Ibid.

6. See, for example, "Political Report of the Embassy of the Soviet Union in the United States for 1947," 25 September 1948, AVP USSR. Fond referentury po USA. Op. 31a, p. I, i. 041, p. 241, l. 1–130.

7. AVP USSR. Fond Arkhivonostravochnaia biblioteka. God 1965. Op. 24-g, p. 19, d. 4, l. 172.

8. Ibid.

Commentary

Melvyn P. Leffler

The document is a tease. Clearly, it was part of an internal policy debate. From Novikov's memoir we know that Molotov encouraged the Washington embassy to send this analysis to Moscow.[1] But no other documents have been made available to illuminate the identities and positions of Molotov's adversaries. To grasp the context of decision making we still need to rely on books by Werner Hahn, William McCagg, Gavriel Ra'anan, Albert Resis, Timothy Dunmore, and other scholars who base their stimulating accounts of infighting in the Kremlin on inadequate source materials.[2] What we do know is that Stalin remained the final arbiter of these debates. And it is interesting and important to note that at the time this telegram arrived in Moscow, and for many months thereafter, Stalin was not yet prepared to accept Novikov's and Molotov's advice and interpretation.[3]

Viewed as part of an internal debate, we should take this telegram seriously. What is most conspicuous, and perhaps least important, is how little it reveals about Soviet foreign policy objectives. Or course, we would not ordinarily expect an embassy analyzing the foreign policy of a host nation to provide extensive policy prescriptions. But Kennan's "Long Telegram," to which Novikov's dispatch is now being compared, provided the basic contours of the containment policy.[4] In contrast, Novikov and his aides say almost nothing about Soviet goals. Should Soviet diplomacy be defensive or offensive? Should it pursue revolutionary objectives or nationalistic ones? Should it support a spheres-of-influence approach or should it be more ambitious and risk taking? Novikov alludes to the postwar disequilibrium in the international system, but says little about the potential for revolutionary successes, Communist party victories, decolonization, and other matters that would be of critical importance to officials in the Kremlin who were making key decisions about Soviet-American relations in the postwar period.

Another conspicuous aspect of Novikov's telegram is the shallow, distorted image it provides of U.S. goals and motivations. The examination is warped by ideology, which rather than being used to provide a systematic and potentially useful framework for interpreting what is going on, serves here as a substitute for thoughtful analysis. The superficial allusions to "imperialistic tendencies," "American monopolistic capital," "ruling classes," "reactionary circles," and "world supremacy" are pathetic, not because they are unworthy of consideration, but because they receive no serious consideration.

Given the ideological assumptions that are stated in the first sentence and that inform everything that follows, it is noteworthy how little effort went into examining the domestic economic scene in the United States. There are no references to the widespread strikes, labor turmoil, housing shortages, and inflationary pressures. There is no analysis of the business cycle, of the prospects for boom and bust, of the possible need to sustain overseas markets after the accumulated savings of the wartime years were spent. Instead, we see only a set of the most vacuous allusions to collaborative efforts between "the far right wing of the Democratic party and the Republican party." How interesting it might have been to see Novikov presenting a penetrating dissection of the American political economy, perhaps even with some attention focused on the rising importance of high tech industries and international banking firms that, some scholars now claim, played a decisive role in the formulation of postwar policy.[5]

Notwithstanding these conspicuous shortcomings, I find Novikov's description of U.S. policies to be considerably more accurate. His account of the Anglo-American relationship—his stress on the cooperative impulses and competitive thrusts—comports with key elements of some of the best historical literature that has been written over the last couple of decades. His understanding of the disruptive role American capital might play within the British Empire coincides with the perceptions of British officials. His allusions to both the formal and informal elements of Anglo-American military cooperation are not very wide of the mark.[6] His concerns about American naval visits to the eastern Mediterranean and Middle East would have made James Forrestal rejoice, for this is precisely how the secretary of the navy intended them to be seen.[7] Forrestal's interest in Middle East oil, and the interest of other leading U.S. officials in this critical resource, is well known, and Novikov correctly outlines the ongoing rivalry of the Americans and the British in this part of the world.[8] At the same time the Soviet diplomat correctly assesses Washington's intention to dominate occupation policy in Japan, to play a key role in China, and to facilitate the return of the British, French, and Dutch to Southeast Asia.[9] And his emphasis on the scope of U.S. overseas base planning and the level of military expenditures, although somewhat imprecise, can be more or less verified in official U.S. records.[10] In this regard it is interesting to note how Novikov compares U.S. military spending to its prewar levels (1938), a comparison that we historians rarely make when we are inclined to contrast the allegedly modest levels of 1946–1949 to the larger budgets that occurred during the Korean War.

Still, we should *not* be overly impressed with Novikov's descriptive abilities. There are grave flaws in his analysis. He overlooks the magnitude of the demobilization effort and disregards the paltry state of U.S. military preparedness in 1946. He errs egregiously in suggesting that high-level civilian policymakers were contemplating something along the lines of a preemptive war. Although correct in citing the presence and importance of U.S. forces in China, he totally misses the fact that the Truman administration was then disengaging from its close association with Chiang Kai-shek's Nationalist cause. Novikov's emphasis on the role of U.S. capital in molding policy toward Palestine is misplaced and his stress on the degree of Anglo-American collaboration on East European questions is overstated. In addition, although it is true that American officials were increasingly rejecting decartelization policies in Germany and Japan and beginning to form alliances with indigenous elites, there was still (in mid-1946) a reformist thrust to occupation practices in defeated Axis countries and a definite preference to work with middle-of-the-road political groupings there and elsewhere.

There is a thread that ties together both the flaws and the insights in Novikov's descriptive account of U.S. policy. Whether he is right or wrong, the matters he discusses illuminate his fears, his perception of threat, and, in a larger context, the Soviet sense of vulnerability. He is afraid of U.S. military power; he is afraid of preemptive war. He is worried that U.S. military bases will encircle the Soviet homeland. He is apprehensive that the stationing of U.S. forces in China could serve as a bridgehead for an offensive against the Soviet Union. He is afraid that the presence of the U.S. navy in the eastern Mediterranean and the projection of American forces into the Middle East portend a new threat to the southern flank of the Soviet Union. He is fearful that the United States will mobilize Japanese and German power against the Soviet Union. Note that rather than welcoming a rapid power termination of the German occupation as an opportunity to expand the Kremlin's influence, he is fearful that the United States is scheming to move in this direction because Washington wants to co-opt German strength for an anti-Soviet coalition. Note, too, that although Novikov stresses Soviet successes in Eastern Europe, he is apprehensive that the United States might dislodge the Russians from their own periphery. His respect for the power of U.S. capital is palpable throughout the telegram; that capital can disrupt the British Empire and penetrate the Soviet sphere of influence. Even inside the United Nations, he sees the United States moving to abolish the veto in the Security Council and working "to impose the will of other countries on the Soviet Union." Not surprisingly, Novikov's conclusion is that the Truman administration has abandoned Roosevelt's cooperating disposition. And in this more competitive context, the Soviet sense of vulnerability becomes all too clear.

Some readers might object to this view and argue that all of the above was a ruse to conceal a more offensive, expansionist, revolutionary foreign policy that the Russians wanted to pursue for their own internal reasons. Such an interpretation is possible, but I see little in this document that would support such a notion. Indeed, returning to where I began, it is surprising how little is said here about what the Kremlin should be doing. Instead, there is an obsessive recounting of American expansionism, distrustfulness, and strategic preparedness—all suggestive of a fear of American economic and military power. And this view, written for internal purposes in 1946, still resonates through some of the memoir literature that the era of *glasnost* is generating. One is struck, for example, to see in *Khrushchev Remembers: The Glasnost Tapes* the following passage: "In the days leading up to Stalin's death, we believed that America would invade the Soviet Union and we would go to war. Stalin trembled at this prospect. How he quivered. He was afraid of war. He knew that we were weaker than the United States. . . . This fear stayed with him from the first days of World War II, when he said: 'Lenin left us a state and we turned it to shit.' Our victory in the war did not stop him from trembling inside."[11]

And similar passages run through Andrei Gromyko's recently published memoir. After World War II, he says, the Americans wanted "to force us to accept their plans on questions affecting Europe and the world." Stalin, Gromyko argues, immediately believed that Truman wanted to use the atomic bomb to intimidate the Soviets and to renege on matters of vital importance to Soviet Russia—for example, the payment of German reparations. "With this weapon in America's hands, Truman evidently felt he could dictate terms to the Soviet Union." Roosevelt's successor, Gromyko writes with controlled contempt, "did nothing to hide his hostility to the power which had borne the heaviest sacrifices in the war against the common enemy."[12]

The point of this is not to suggest that these descriptions of American policies are accurate. The point is that Soviet leaders did distrust and did fear the United States, and that such fears increased proclivities to distort information and events. A good example of this is apparent in Novikov's own telegram. Toward the very end of his dispatch he says that reputable organs of the American press were advocating war. Even Walter Lippmann, he reports, was calling on the United States "to launch a strike against the Soviet Union in the most vulnerable areas of the south and southeast of the USSR."

Lippmann, in fact, had argued in his column on 7 September 1946 that the United States should build up its power in the eastern Mediterranean, "where, if war comes, the Soviet Union would from the outset be on the defensive." From this location the United States could launch air and sea attacks on "the vital center of Russia." Lippmann also talked of waging war against the Soviet Union, although for him it was a "diplomatic war." The United

States, he argued on 19 September 1946, "should confront power with power at a selected point where a decision is in a military sense possible, and then to use the delicate and unstable equilibrium as an opportunity to be seized for constructive and magnanimous negotiation."[13]

Did Novikov purposefully distort Lippmann? Or did his own sense of Soviet vulnerability incline him to distort the meaning of Lippmann's columns? Or did he fear that if the two powers sat down to discuss the great issues that divided them, they might not agree? If that should occur, an escalatory crisis might unfold and war could come. And in that situation, he could foresee that the Soviet Union might indeed be terribly vulnerable precisely where Lippmann indicated it would be, that is, in the south. Hence he concluded his entire telegram with an emphasis on American preparations for war.

Looking at this document one can see the contradictions and ambiguities in the Soviet position. On the one hand, they have achieved great successes; on the other hand, they see threats everywhere. On the one hand, they have strengthened their defensive perimeter; on the other hand, they are vulnerable to American air and sea power, which is increasingly ensconced in overseas bases, in the eastern Mediterranean, and in northeast Asia. On the one hand, they can remain economically independent of the outside world; on the other hand, American capital has the potential to penetrate the economies and overthrow the governments of the Kremlin's "democratic" allies in Eastern Europe.

If this document is revealing for what it implicitly says about the Soviet sense of vulnerability, it is equally revealing for its indifference to and disregard for American threat perceptions. For although Novikov was right to stress American financial power and *potential* military capabilities, he totally overlooks Americans' sense of their own vulnerability in an international system that had just gone through fifteen years of world depression and global war. Truman and his advisers knew that the country was very powerful but they also faced grave perils: Soviet aggrandizement in Eastern Europe and northeast Asia; prospects for Communist party victories in France, Italy, and Greece; uncertainties about the future orientation of Germany and Japan; civil war in China; revolutionary nationalist ferment in southeast Asia. From Novikov's telegram, no one would have any inkling that such fears plagued the Washington policymaking community.

So here we can see how one's own fears and vulnerabilities incapacitate one's ability to assess accurately the fears, motives, and vulnerabilities of one's adversary.[14] And I would suggest that this shortcoming afflicted American assessments of Soviet intentions and capabilities just as much as it afflicted Soviet assessments of American intentions and capabilities. But alas, this is another story for another time.[15]

Notes

1. Comments of Soviet historian Vladimir Zubok at a meeting of the Institute for Policy Studies, Washington, 28 March 1991.

2. Werner G. Hahn, *Postwar Soviet Politics: The Fall of Zhdanov and the Defeat of Moderation* (Ithaca, 1982); William O. McCagg, *Stalin Embattled, 1943–1948* (Detroit, 1978); Gavriel D. Ra'anan, *International Policy Formation in the U.S.S.R.: Factional "Debates" during the Zhdanovschina* (Hamden, CT, 1983); Albert Resis, *Stalin, the Politburo, and the Onset of the Cold War* (Pittsburgh, 1988); Timothy Dunmore, *Soviet Politics, 1945–1953* (London, 1983).

3. For the ambiguities and evolution of Stalin's policies see William Taubman, *Stalin's American Policy: From Entente to Détente to Cold War* (New York, 1982).

4. See Kenneth M. Jensen, ed., *Origins of the Cold War: The Novikov, Kennan, and Roberts "Long Telegrams" of 1946* (Washington, 1991).

5. See, for example, Thomas Ferguson, "From Normalcy to New Deal: Industrial Structure, Party Competition, and American Public Policy in the Great Depression," *International Organization* 38 (Winter 1984): 41–94.

6. For Anglo-American relations see, for example, Robert M. Hathaway, *Ambiguous Partnership: Britain and America, 1944–1947* (New York, 1981); Terry H. Anderson, *The United States, Great Britain, and the Cold War, 1944–1947* (Columbia, MO, 1981); Richard A. Best, Jr., *"Cooperation with Like-Minded Peoples": British Influences on American Security Policy, 1945–1949* (Westport, CT, 1986); Wm. Roger Louis, *The British Empire in the Middle East, 1945–1951: Arab Nationalism, the United States, and Postwar Imperialism* (New York, 1984); Michael J. Hogan, *The Marshall Plan: America, Britain, and the Reconstruction of Western Europe, 1947–1952* (New York, 1987); and Randall Woods, *A Changing of the Guard: Anglo-American Relations, 1941–1946* (Chapel Hill, 1991).

7. Walter Millis, ed., *The Forrestal Diaries* (New York, 1951), 141, 144–145, 171, 184, 187, 196, 211, 258, 302.

8. Michael Stoff, *Oil, War, and American Security: The Search for a National Policy on Foreign Oil, 1941–1947* (New Haven, 1980); Aaron David Miller, *Search for Security: Saudi Arabian Oil and American Foreign Policy, 1939–1949* (Chapel Hill, 1980); Irvine H. Anderson, *Aramco, the United States, and Saudi Arabia: A Study in the Dynamics of Foreign Oil Policy, 1933–1950* (Princeton, 1981); David S. Painter, *Oil and the American Century: The Political Economy of U.S. Foreign Oil Policy, 1941–1954* (Baltimore, 1986).

9. See, for example, Marc S. Gallicchio, *The Cold War Begins in Asia: American East Asian Policy and the Fall of the Japanese Empire* (New York, 1988); Howard B. Schonberger, *Aftermath of War: Americans and the Remaking of Japan* (Kent, OH, 1989); Michael Schaller, *The American Occupation of Japan: The Origins of the Cold War in Asia* (New York, 1985); and Robert J. McMahon, *Colonialism and Cold War: The United States and the Struggle for Indonesian Independence, 1945–1949* (Ithaca, 1981).

10. For base planning see the Records of the Joint Chiefs of Staff, RG 218, CCS 360 (12-9-42), National Archives, Washington.

11. *Khrushchev Remembers: The Glasnost Tapes* (Boston, 1990), 100–101.

12. Andrei Gromyko, *Memoirs* (New York, 1989), 96–110 (with the quotations on pp. 96 and 110).

13. *New York Herald Tribune*, 7 and 19 September 1946.

14. For some insights on the relationship between cognition and threat perception see Robert Jervis, Richard Ned Lebow, and Janice Gross Stein, *Psychology and Deterrence* (Baltimore, 1985).

15. See my book *A Preponderance of Power: National Security, the Truman Administration, and the Cold War* (Stanford, 1992).

Commentary

Steven Merritt Miner

During Winston Churchill's visit to Moscow in October 1944, he learned that Josef Stalin still harbored dark suspicions about Rudolph Hess's flight to Britain in May 1941. The prime minister tried unsuccessfully to reassure his host by explaining that there had never been any reason to fear an Anglo-German separate peace. Stalin flatly rejected Churchill's assurances; although he professed to accept that the prime minister had not personally entered into negotiations with the deputy führer, and that he was even perhaps unaware of any such dealings, he refused to believe that nobody in the British government had discussed peace terms with Hess. "There are lots of things that happen even here in Russia," Stalin said, "which our Secret Service do not necessarily tell me about." Recalling this exchange after the war, Churchill wrote that "remembering what a wise man [Stalin] is, I was surprised to find him silly on this point."[1]

The Soviet dictator's musings about Hess may indeed have been misplaced, but his remark about the unreliability of information provided by subordinates highlights a familiar dilemma besetting any dictator. A despot enjoying the power of life and death over his underlings, Stalin nonetheless was in many respects a prisoner of the information those below him chose to provide. Before historians can hope to write an adequate history of Soviet foreign policy, they must first discover what Soviet leaders knew, or were told, about the world beyond the Soviet Union's borders.

My first reaction on receiving the Novikov document was excitement; at long last *glasnost* would lead to the opening of Soviet archives, and historians would now be able to write the history of the Cold War from the other side. We would finally be able to begin to assess Soviet motives, see how the Soviets perceived the outside world, and answer one of the central conundrums of Soviet history: How did official Marxism-Leninism shape, or warp, Soviet perceptions and actions? Clearly, this enthusiasm was a common reaction. The Novikov document is easily compared with George Kennan's "Long Telegram," and this symposium itself suggests that we are eager to see it in this light.

After reading and rereading Novikov's analysis many times, however, familiar concerns resurface, and old caution flags spring up. The suspicious tone of Novikov's writing, his underlying assumption that the outside world was unremittingly hostile toward the Soviet Union, and his crude economic explanations for complex events leave us with nagging questions: Did he really see the world in these terms? Did his bosses back in Moscow? Was he simply telling them what he thought they wanted to hear? The sad fact is that this single document snatched from the Soviet archives does not take us much further along the road toward confident answers. In our eagerness finally to get at the truths of Soviet foreign policy, we must not load more ballast into this small vessel than it will ship. Our resources for writing the history of Soviet diplomacy remain pitifully slim; by way of analogy, one should imagine the daunting task of writing a history of American postwar foreign policy based solely on Kennan's "Long Telegram" and scattered official State Department publications.

We do know certain useful facts about the document: that V. M. Molotov commissioned the analysis, that he did so in the wake of the rancorous foreign ministers' conference in Paris that dragged on fruitlessly through the summer of 1946, and that he apparently read and underlined certain passages. The underlined sections themselves would also seem to support what has long been known about Molotov—that he was always ready to view Western actions in the least favorable, most conspiratorial light.

Beyond this, we know very little. Who, other than Molotov, read the memorandum; how did the document's analysis alter the course of Soviet foreign policy, if at all; what other sources of information did Soviet leaders have for a fuller understanding of American motives; were these other sources as wedded as Novikov apparently was to a Stalinist analysis of the world situation, or did the Soviet leadership have access to a spectrum of views? Was the document a genuine analysis at all, or rather a position piece designed to establish the Communist line for the Soviet Union's East European satraps? These are not idle questions, because in writing diplomatic history context is nearly everything. Kennan's "Long Telegram" is not important because of its style, elegant though it may be. Nor was Kennan's analysis entirely novel; Loy Henderson, Charles Bohlen, and others had said many similar things earlier. The document is important because, from the cacophony of voices trumpeting interpretations of Soviet postwar foreign policy through the halls of power in postwar Washington, Kennan's clear tones struck a sympathetic chord with both the government and the public. We know nothing yet about the reception accorded Novikov's memorandum. It may indeed have been a critical document; it may just as well be the sort of year-end summary of the host nation's policies that every embassy files, only to collect dust in the archives.

If we can only guess about the memorandum's importance, there is ample historical reason to be cautious about uncritically accepting the author's analytical framework or conclusions as a genuine reflection of his own views. The historian of Russia and the Soviet Union encounters a recurrent pattern that may bear on this matter: The authoritarian governments of the tsars, and later of the commissars, suffered chronically from an information blockage. In theory, an authoritarian state should function in such a way that the leader at the apex of power receives unadulterated information, which enables him or her to issue orders addressing foreign and domestic problems. In practice, however, the system has rarely worked as intended; lacking channels of information independent of the state apparatus, Russian leaders have often been cut off from reliable information, as Stalin's remarks cited above attest. This was as true of Nicholas I as it was for Yuri Andropov. Russia's rulers have tried various palliatives for this persistent ailment: The more dictatorial among them created ever-more sections of the secret police or intelligence services to monitor the other branches of government to assure that they were working properly. Aleksandr II, and Mikhail Gorbachev, by contrast, realized that the only solution to the problem lies in greater openness.

Stalin's government suffered from increasingly adulterated information, so much so that toward the end of his life the dictator became trapped in an echo chamber of his own making, where every voice reaching his ears was in fact his own. Numerous articles have appeared in the Soviet press during the last several years showing how factory managers, party bosses, and other officials all routinely doctored statistics to persuade their superiors that unfulfilled plans had been exceeded, that failed harvests were bountiful, and so forth. They did this from sheer terror, fearing the dreadful consequence of failing to meet unrealistic goals set by state and party authorities.

These same dynamics prevailed in foreign affairs and intelligence, often with dire consequences for the Soviet people. The best-documented and most disastrous incident of this sort was Stalin's failure to heed the scores of warnings he received about Hitler's invasion plans in 1941.[2] Stalin actually ordered one particularly persistent intelligence chief, Lieutenant General Proskurin, executed when the latter continued to warn of a German attack after Stalin had labeled such theories British disinformation.[3] Given our ignorance of such matters, we can only guess as to the overall impact of Stalin's terror on the quality of information he received from his agents and diplomats abroad. Although no clear pattern is readily discernible in the ruthless purging of the foreign commissariat during the years 1938–39,[4] it is reasonable to assume that purge survivors were imbued with a sense of caution and tailored their dispatches to conform with what they believed their bosses wanted to hear. In 1946, as the relatively more open character of the wartime Soviet Union was once again squeezed into the xenophobic Stalinist mold, it would have taken a very brave diplomat indeed to present the Soviet Foreign Ministry with an analysis of American foreign policy in the postwar world that attributed anything but the most discreditable motives to Washington.

In addition to instilling a stifling caution into the average Soviet diplomat, the purges had another long-lasting effect. In the first years following the Bolshevik Revolution, the Foreign Commissariat had been able to draw on a deep well of personnel familiar with the outside world and fluent in foreign languages.

Many Russian revolutionaries had lived abroad during years of forced exile, awaiting the overthrow of the tsarist autocracy. This group formed the nucleus of the infant Bolshevik foreign service; such early Soviet diplomatic luminaries as Boris Chicherin, Maksim Litvinov, and Ivan Maiskii were only the best-known representatives of this generation. The purges thinned the ranks of this cosmopolitan diplomatic corps, replacing veterans with a flood of novices; from the late Stalinist period extending well into Leonid Brezhnev's time, the average diplomat's career had begun no earlier than 1938. Nor was the training of this new generation in any way impressive: By way of example, the most famous of this class of '38–'39, Andrei Gromyko, was trained in economics. He did not even know a foreign language when he received his first posting broad, to Washington on the eve of the war.[5]

The selection of such a novice for so important a posting suggests that Stalin, or his close partner in foreign affairs at that time, Molotov, actually selected such newcomers for sensitive positions believing that their lack of experience, far from harming Soviet diplomacy, would in fact make them loyal executors of policies dictated from Moscow. For a time during the war, from 1941 to 1943, the widely experienced Litvinov was plucked from obscurity and appointed ambassador to Washington. But by his own account in various conversations with Western diplomats, Litvinov was not listened to in Moscow nor were his hands free in Washington. As he told American undersecretary of state Sumner Welles: "He had even been forbidden to appear in public or to make any public speeches"; furthermore, he complained that Molotov "had removed from the Foreign Commissariat every important official who had any experience with the outside world and any personal knowledge of the . . . Western democracies."[6]

In 1943 the Soviets withdrew Litvinov from Washington and Maiskii from London. With their removal, the conduct of Soviet foreign policy in the Western democracies fell into the hands of people who knew little about the workings of non-Soviet societies, people who owed their newfound prominence to the purging of their predecessors and who can thus be assumed to have been highly reticent to say a good word about the "bourgeois" powers—even if they knew very much about them at all. Judging by the few accounts we have of life in Soviet embassies, the inhabitants of these hothouse transplants from Stalin's jungle were not allowed to learn much about the societies to which they were posted, for fear of their becoming contaminated by Western ways.[7]

This brings us back to Novikov's memorandum. The document contains some shrewd observations, particularly about the strains in the Anglo-American partnership and the possible threat posed to the Soviet Union by the new string of U.S. bases springing up around the world in the wake of the war. Along with such insights, however, Novikov wrote a good deal of nonsense: Only someone dreadfully ignorant of American society, or blinkered by Marxist analysis, could argue, for instance, that American policy toward Jewish migration to Israel was determined solely, or even primarily, by economic considerations. Even more important were the features of the Soviet-American relationship that Novikov did not even choose to mention: He made no effort to analyze how Soviet policy, particularly in Eastern Europe, was fanning the flames of Washington's suspicions of Stalin.

Were these omissions or misinterpretations the result of ignorance, inexperience, or blinkered reasoning? Or was Novikov mindful of his predecessors' fate and thus reticent about telling Moscow what he knew to be true? Without further evidence we cannot answer these questions. Nor can we judge how representative this memorandum is of Soviet documentation as a whole. Why was this one document released? Because it is one of the most insightful, influential documents of its kind? Or because it is precisely the opposite? Did its release serve the interests of one particular faction in a bureaucratic fight in Moscow? If so, was it designed to show just how crude Soviet diplomatic reasoning was at the time, or to illustrate how the Soviets genuinely did fear American power? We do know that in today's turbulent Moscow various political factions, representing trends ranging from old-line Stalinist to genuinely democratic, are fighting historical battles, using documents as ammunition. Is this one fusillade from this skirmishing?

The Novikov document raises more questions than it answers. If we are truly to understand the history of Soviet foreign policy we will need more than the release of a single memorandum each year—or decade—no matter how important. Until we do receive access to more information, we can only recall Stalin's insight that all information is incomplete, and some is even intentionally misleading.

Notes

1. Winston S. Churchill, *The Grand Alliance* (Boston, 1950), 55.

2. For an excellent discussion of Stalin's refusal to heed such warnings see Barton Whaley, *Codeword Barbarossa* (Cambridge, MA, 1973).

3. Petro Grigorenko, *Memoirs*, trans. Thomas P. Whitney (New York, 1982), 115–121.

4. See Teddy J. Uldricks, "The Impact of the Purges on the People's Commissariat of Foreign Affairs," *Slavic Review* 36 (June 1977): 187–204. By contrast, Evgenil Gnedin, who was himself a victim of the purge in the Foreign Commissariat, has argued that the purges were directed at both Jews and at genuine Communists who were uneasy with Stalin's cooperation with Nazi Germany. See Gnedin, *Katastrofa i vtoroe rozhdenie* [Disaster and rebirth] (Amsterdam, 1977).

5. A. A. Gromyko et al., eds., *Diplomaticheskii slovar'* [Diplomatic dictionary], vol. 1 (Moscow, 1985), 275–276. See also Gromyko, *Pamiatnoe* [Memorial], vol. 1 (Moscow, 1988).

6. Welles memorandum, 7 May 1943, U.S. Department of State, *Foreign Relations of the United States, 1943* (Washington, 1963), 3:522–524.

7. See, for example, Victor Kravchenko, *I Chose Freedom* (New York, 1946), 455–472. Although perhaps unreliable in some particulars, Kravchenko's account of the atmosphere within a Soviet embassy is substantiated by other defectors' accounts.

United States Institute of Peace

The United States Institute of Peace is an independent, nonpartisan federal institution created and funded by Congress to strengthen the nation's capacity to promote the peaceful resolution of international conflict. Established in 1984, the Institute meets its congressional mandate through an array of programs, including grants, fellowships, conferences and workshops, library services, publications, and other educational activities. The Institute's Board of Directors is appointed by the President of the United States and confirmed by the Senate.

Board of Directors

Research and Studies Program

To complement its research grants and fellowships for organizations and individuals, the United States Institute of Peace established its own Research and Studies Program in 1988.

Research and Studies projects are designed and directed by the Institute, which supervises their implementation with the assistance of expert consultants and contract researchers. Most projects are carried out through a process that includes the production of working papers on a selected topic and discussion of them by experts in public session. Proceedings from the sessions are redrafted as papers, reports, articles, monographs, and books to assist scholars, educators, journalists, policymakers, and citizens' groups in understanding issues of peace and war.

Research and Studies activities fall into four main categories: study groups, public workshops, working group projects, and studies. Study groups run from four to six months and involve a core group of expert participants in intensive examination of near-term international conflict situations. Public workshops are two- to three-hour events designed for group discussion around a discrete topic of current concern. Working group projects run for one year or longer and proceed through four or more public sessions involving a core group of expert participants. Studies are conceived on the same scale as working groups, but with a changing cast of participants. In all these activities, the Institute strives to provide for representation of a wide range of viewpoints and to address its mandate to contribute to and disseminate knowledge about ways of achieving peace by doing as much work as possible in public session.

Kenneth M. Jensen
Director

9836